Reclaiming the Power

The How and Why of Practical Ritual Magic

Lady Sabrina

One of the most usable and workable approaches to magic ever written . . .

For more than a decade, Lady Sabrina has been teaching people about magic. Not a select few who have been screened for the purpose, but ordinary individuals, with ordinary problems, who are looking for simple and reasonable solutions. Many people have absolutely no idea what the Qabalah or Western Magic is and could care less in the face of crisis. They don't have the time or inclination to get involved with a specific tradition such as Wicca or Paganism. They just want something they can understand and work with that will get results.

Getting results is what *Reclaiming the Power* is all about. The average person can take this book, read it and apply its concepts to his or her daily life. If there is something you need or want, this book explains in simple terms how to get it. But, most importantly, it teaches you along the way that you *can* do it. It shows you how to get back your self-confidence, self-esteem and personal power . . . *for it is these very qualities that not only make magic work—THEY MAKE LIFE WORK AS WELL!*

Many books on the subject of magic have been written for the accomplished occultist. These are wonderful for the esoteric and profound, but for the individual who just wants a job promotion they are meaningless. *Reclaiming the Power* is different. There are no eighty-dollar words, complicated rituals or magical processes that only genius can understand. Just the simple, straightforward approach to magic that anyone can use.

This book is long overdue and definitely relevant in these changing times. After all, change is what magic is all about.

About the Author

Lady Sabrina, born an Aquarius in Kansas City, Missouri, has been actively involved in Wicca and the magical arts for the past 15 years. Sabrina has spent a great deal of time studying various spiritual paths and researching major world religions—including druidism, shamanism, voodoo, Latin American magic and European Witchcraft.

In 1978, Sabrina founded Our Lady of Enchantment, a church and school of the Old Religion. It is a Wiccan Metaphysical Center, and is open to the public. Sabrina has written and prepared all of the school's correspondence courses, the on-campus classes, workshops, and the bi-monthly newsletter. She facilitates the worship services offered by the school.

Lady Sabrina's expertise on the subject of magic and pre-Christian religious systems has been acknowledged by the metaphysical community as well as the national media. She has appeared on such shows as *Phil Donahue, Geraldo, People Are Talking, Crossroads, In Question, New Hampshire Journal, The Look Show* and *The World of People,* as well as various evening news programs, and dozens of live radio talk shows.

Sabrina is an initiated High Priestess and a legally recognized minister of Wicca. She regularly lectures at colleges, leads public ceremonies, and performs handfastings, rites of passage, and other rituals.

To Write to the Author

Both the author and the publisher appreciate hearing from readers, and learning of your enjoyment and benefit from this book. The author participates in seminars and workshops. She also conducts correspondence courses. To write to the author, or to ask a question, write to:

Lady Sabrina
P. O. Box 1366
Nashua, NH 03061, U.S.A.

Free Catalog From Llewellyn

For more than 90 years Llewellyn has brought its readers knowledge in the fields of metaphysics and human potential. Learn about the newest books in spiritual guidance, natural healing, astrology, occult philosophy and more. Enjoy book reviews, new age articles, a calendar of events, plus current advertised products and services. To get your free copy of the *New Times,* send your name and address to:

The Llewellyn New Times
P. O. Box 64383–166, St. Paul, MN 55164–0383, U.S.A.

Llewellyn's Practical Guide to Personal Power

Reclaiming the Power

The How and Why
of
Practical Ritual Magic

by
Lady Sabrina

1992
Llewellyn Publications
St. Paul, Minnesota, 55164–0383, U.S.A.

FIRST EDITION, 1992

Cover painting by Randy Asplund-Faith
Photos by Stasia Millet
Illustrations by Lady Sabrina and Lisa Peschel

Library of Congress Cataloging-in-Publication Data
Sabrina, Lady.
    Reclaiming the power: the how and why of practical ritual magic / by Lady Sabrina.
        p.   cm.   —   (Llewellyn's practical guide to personal power)
    ISBN 0–87542–166–0
    1. Magic.   2. Ritual.   I. Title.   II. Series.
BF1623.R6S33   1992
133.4′3—dc20   92–8696
                                                                    CIP

Llewellyn Publications
A Division of Llewellyn Worldwide, Ltd.
P.O. Box 64383, St. Paul, MN 55164-0383

About the Llewellyn Practical Guides to Personal Power

To some people, the idea that "magick" is *practical* comes as a surprise. It shouldn't!

The entire basis for magick is to exercise influence over one's personal world in order to satisfy our needs and goals. And, while this magick is also concerned with psychological transformation and spiritual growth, even the spiritual life must be built on firm material foundations.

Here are practical and usable techniques that will help you to a better life, will help you attain things you want, will help you in your personal growth and development. *Moreover, these books can change your life, dynamically, positively!*

The material world and the psychic are intertwined, and it is this that establishes the magickal link: that mind/soul/spirit can as easily influence the material as vice versa.

Psychic powers and magickal practices can, and should, be used in one's daily life. Each of us has many wonderful, yet underdeveloped talents and powers—surely we have an evolutionary obligation to make full use of our human potentials! Mind and body work together, and magick is simply the extension of this interaction into dimensions beyond the limits normally conceived. *Why be limited?*

All things you will ever want or be must have their start in your mind. In these books you are given practical guidance to develop your inner powers and apply them to your everyday needs. These abilities will eventually belong to everybody through natural evolution, but you can learn and develop them now!

This series of books will help you achieve such things as success, happiness, miracles, powers of ESP, healing, out-of-body travel, clairvoyance, divination, extended powers of mind and body, communication with non-physical beings and knowledge by non-material means!

We've always known of things like this . . . seemingly supernormal achievements, often by quite ordinary people. We are told that we normally use only ten percent of our human potential. We are taught that faith can move mountains, that love heals all hurt, that miracles do occur. We believe these things to be true, but most people lack practical knowledge of them.

The books in this series form a full library of magickal knowledge and practice.

Forthcoming Books by the Author

Earth, Religion, and Power:
How to Create Your Own Spiritual Path

Santeria: Diary of an Initiate

Dedication

I dedicate this book to the members and students of Our Lady Of Enchantment Church, and especially to Balaam, Cassius, Galadriel, Bob, Ellen, Beth, Garb, Pat, Dick, Paul and all those who have volunteered their time, energy and effort over the years. In appreciation for my early teachings I thank Lady Sintana, Bob and Dorothy, Herman Slater, Janice and Dee Dee.

Special thanks go to Nancy Mostad, Deborah Chapdelaine and the Staff of Llewellyn, who are responsible for this book coming to life so quickly.

—— CONTENTS ——

—— INTRODUCTION ——

On August 16th, 1987, thousands of people from all over the world gathered together. Some were party to well-coordinated seminars, others just assembled in small intimate groups. Whether encircled on a mountain top or cloistered in a hidden valley, young and old, black and white, all stood united, welcoming in the New Age. This monumental occasion was called the Harmonic Convergence[1], and it brought the essence of the Aquarian Era to the forefront of the world's consciousness.

The Harmonic Convergence was a conscious bonding of people; an evolutionary shift from separation to unity, and from fear to love. The time had come to drop old hatreds, artificial boundaries and fundamental prejudices. Race, color and creed had no meaning during this period of unified transformation.

For many, the Harmonic Convergence was the crossover point from the Piscian Age to the Age of Aquarius—a fleeting moment when gender and demeanor were not important but the appreciation of collective consciousness was. During this brief segment of time, the New Aeon was felt within and expressed outwardly through various means of ritual. It really didn't matter where you were, or what you were doing, the energy was there and the Harmonic Convergence did happen.

---

[1] It is the time the Maya, Hopi and Tibetans historically set for the change of energy frequency at primary lay junctions. This was the beginning of the change of the harmonic resonance of the electromagnetic field of the earth. It is the change from one great era to another.

With the passing of the Convergence we saw a very dramatic change take place. Although the level of energy was subtle, the results were not, and the New Age thundered to the forefront of our consciousness. Suddenly the entire world was aware of something other than the material pursuits of the past few decades. Magic, metaphysics, the Goddess and Neo-Paganism were not merely topics of discussion, they were producing alternative life styles.

People began to discover there were other philosophies, spiritual paths and ways of doing things. No longer were you an outcast if you did not follow in the footsteps of your father, mother, or brother. The New Age and its unusual and curious ways were being promoted by movie stars, book publishers, clothing companies, and by a good majority of the retail market. In one way or another, everyone has been affected by the New Age movement to some extent.

Change is what the New Age movement is all about. Whether we agree with this or not really doesn't matter. The New Age is here and so are the changes it has brought with it. One of these changes is the belief in personal power—the power to create at will and bring into manifestation what we desire. This power is what occultists call magic.

Magic and change are intertwined, as magic causes change to occur. However, when a change occurs as the result of magic, it is not spontaneous; it is controlled and calculated. Through the realization of personal accomplishment, magic helps restore individual self-esteem and confidence. This renewed belief in one's own personal power leads to a more productive life.

When people begin to realize they have control over their own destinies, they are more willing to accept responsibility for their actions. They are not only able to help themselves but are in a position to help others as well.

When this happens, people find that they are moving and working in harmony with their surroundings, completing a cycle[2], and contributing to the present-day social structure.

Unfortunately, qualities like self-esteem, self-confidence and the knowledge of personal power have to be dealt with on an individual basis. There is no one, true, right and only answer for us collectively. This is why the philosophies of the New Age, the Magical Lodges, and resurgence of Wicca[3] are so relevant at this time. They provide the individual with the necessary tools to make changes and allow for the personal expression of inner spiritual feelings.

The purpose of this book is to show how magic can be used through traditional ceremony to accomplish personal goals. By learning to work with the flow of universal power we are better able to channel and focus our energy in a constructive manner.

Magic is not complicated. It is not without structural reason nor is it in opposition to nature. In fact, it is just the opposite. Magic teaches us that by aligning ourselves with the natural flow of the universe, through reasonable methods, we can simply and effortlessly get what we need and want. All it really takes is some imagination, the desire to change, and a willingness to consider what most people don't understand.

---

[2] Here the word cycle refers to a series of occurrences which repeat themselves in specific patterns, thus allowing the individual to progress and grow materially as well spiritually.

[3] An Anglo-Saxon term meaning "Wise One," currently Witchcraft; a Pagan religion with pre-Christian ties to folk magic, and a belief in both a God and Goddess.Wicca celebrates seasonal rites.

PART I
MAGIC AND RITUAL

CHAPTER ONE

The Definition of Magic

A Desire to Change

Just what is magic? Is it an illusion, or is there some basis for its existence? Can anyone do it? Is it good or evil? Can you prove that magic really works? Isn't magic just positive thinking? These are just some of the questions I have been asked by both seeker and skeptic.

To begin with, magic is a process through which the individual causes changes to occur in accordance with his or her own will. It is considered by most of its practitioners to be a tool, as well as a process. This tool or process is used to manipulate the energy and forces of the universe in order to bend reality.

Magic is something everyone can do and is only as good, or evil, as the individual using it. Magic really does work. However, it can only be proved in retrospect because it is not instantaneous. It works through symbols and channels of consciousness. Because magic utilizes all three planes of existence—the spiritual, the mental and the physical—it is more than just positive thinking.

Magic, like any philosophy, has infinite possibilities as well as distinct limitations. It relies heavily on the

3

strength of character and mental ability of the individual using it. Probably the most limiting factors in magic are those of fear and frustration. Obstacles such as these are created by lack of knowledge and experience. We only fear what we do not understand.

Frustration is created through lack of experience. Both fear and frustration can be brought under control with training and practice. However, they can never be totally eliminated because of their relationship to our survival. The key here is *they can be controlled*.

Magic is one of the best ways to gain control and bring harmony back into your life. It is what unleashes your personal power and divine spark. Magic allows you, as an individual, to create or bring into physical reality what you most desire. All anyone needs to make magic work for them is an open mind, some basic understanding of universal principles, and a willingness to experiment.

Magic is a process and a tool which will move or bend reality. Magic is equivalent to change and our ability to alter reality. Why the emphasis on change? It is because nothing ever stays the same! All matter is in a constant state of motion. We need only to look back a few years to see how everything has changed. How many of us are still wearing the same clothes we did a year ago? If they have not worn out, they are definitely out of style. The same thing is usually true of our friends, some are still around, some have moved and new ones have come on the scene. We change jobs, houses, cars and attitudes. Consciously or unconsciously we all move with the flow of the current trend. What was important to most of us five years ago is (more than likely) less than a memory today.

Magic can help us make changes and aid in solving impossible situations. Regrettably, magic has usually been kept a highly guarded secret by those who really understand it. What has managed to surface has been so muddled or intellectually confusing that most people shrug it off as superstitious nonsense. Consequently, the power and possibilities of this wonderful tool have been either denied or rejected by the vast majority.

> ### *Magic is real and magic works.*

Magic is not harmful, sinful or complicated. Magic is a tool and one that can be easily used by anyone wishing to create change. You simply must have the desire to make or change something. Unfortunately, change can be a very frightening thing when you come face to face with it. We all get accustomed to the way things are, and we get comfortable with being able to perceive the outcome of our actions. This ability to predict, and therefore deal with the outcome of a situation ceases when we change the surrounding circumstances.

Just think how many times you have seen your friends trapped in undesirable situations. You wonder why they don't do something about it. They don't do something to change it, even though the situation at hand is uncomfortable, because at least they know where it is going and how to deal with it. To change this would bring in all sorts of unknown factors, factors with which they think they might not be able to cope.

Unknown Factors Create Fear

Fear of change, fear of the unknown, or just plain fear keeps many of us locked away in our own personal prisons. Magic can free us from these self-created cells by restoring our self-esteem and confidence. It teaches us through minor accomplishments that we can do it. Most importantly, magic teaches us that we can do it alone. We have everything we need inside, we just need to learn how to bring it out and use it.

The vast majority of people who get into magic do so secretly, and because of this their accomplishments are their own. Personal accomplishment is a very important aspect of magic and is the beginning of recognition of personal power. Nothing can replace the inner awareness of "I did it, and I did it all by myself." This is truly an awakening experience for those who have been conditioned to believe they aren't capable of doing anything, let alone getting what they want.

However, like anything, there are certain rules and principles which govern the movement of magic. These rules are not complex or without reason, they are just good, common sense. Unfortunately, common sense is something we all lack when the "I want it now" mentally takes over. The one differentiating factor with magic, compared to other philosophical or metaphysical applications, is that it will allow your obsession to manifest. Getting what we think we want is sometimes a necessary evil.

We are all here to learn and learn we will, one way or the other. It is as if we never really get out of school. We just graduate from one grade to another. Each brings with it teachers, lessons, tests, accomplishments and disappointments. The effort we put into study and research, and then how we apply what we have learned determines our final grade. This is where magic comes in. It makes the learning easier, the lessons more profitable, and the outcome one of our choosing.

How Magic Works

Magic works by removing what is unwanted from our lives and then filling in the space with something that is wanted. Everyone knows that you can only have one object in one space at a time. This is true of both tangible objects as well as intangible ones. Thoughts are the objects of our desires; they have form and take up space. If we get rid of the undesirable thoughts, we will have room for the beneficial thoughts. We all see successful people and wish we were like them. We can be, just by changing our attitudes and taking chances on new and different things. In fact, when you think about it, you can't be sure that the successful people you admire didn't use magic to get what they now have.

The Characteristics of Magic

The most important factor in all magical operations is the rule of *resolution through frustration*. This means that when all of the conceivable physical methods of obtaining something have failed, we then enlist the powers of magic. We must exhaust all of the possible ways of getting what we want first. It is the frustration of working for something and not being able to get it which raises the psychic energy level.

In addition to the law of resolution through frustration there is another control factor: *the path of least resistance*. This means that magic will travel towards its goal on the most natural, effortless course possible, like water or electricity. Magic avoids tipping the scales of fate and karma which invariably generate a coincidence response.

For those of you who ritually attempt to conjure up your dream mate, be aware that he or she will not fall from the sky into your arms. More than likely (s)he will bump into you on the street or at your place of work. The winning lottery number will not miraculously appear inscribed upon your wall, though it may surface during a dream. This is all part of the way magic works, it avoids opposition and creates the desired effect. It really doesn't matter in the scheme of things how or why magic works, all that really counts is that it does work to bring about the desired result.

Of equal importance is the rule or law of *origination through passion*. This is what will actually bring into manifestation your desires and is the determining factor of whether or not your magic will work. Do you really need those things that you think you want or think you should have? In other words can you live without what you are lusting after? More than likely you can and have been doing so for a long time. This is important, because actual need will influence the amount of energy you are able to produce at any one given time. This in turn will directly influence the magical work itself.

> *Origination through passion means*
> *the available energy is equivalent to desire.*

The line between need and want is very fine. Often it is difficult, if not down right impossible to distinguish requirements from indulgences. There is nothing wrong with wanting or acquiring material pleasures as long as you keep your perspective. This is one aspect of magic that so many aspiring magicians seem to overlook or disregard.

For some reason, humankind has never been able to maintain its equilibrium when it comes to desire versus need. Humans will either totally abstain from all types of physical gratification or indulge their fleshly whims to the point of avarice or greed. Somewhere in between these two opposites is a point of balance where the individual will discover true happiness.

Don't make the mistake of thinking that denial of the physical will bring forth spiritual illumination; in fact, just the opposite will occur. Lack of proper nourishment, continued sexual frustration, sweat, or goose bumps—none of these produce enlightenment. What this type of abstinence does generate is unnatural obsessions, which in the long run can destroy the true spirit of the individual. The same is true of those who rationalize their extravagances, thinking they can outwit the system. Everyone has to answer for their actions, no matter what muddled excuse is forthcoming.

It is important to realize early on just how powerful magic can be. There is an old adage "Be careful what you ask for, you just may get it." Sometimes what we think we want is not necessarily what we really need. The higher self[1] knows what is best and has the unique ability of controlling or rationing out levels of personal energy. This can be very upsetting for those with unyielding passions. If the higher self holds back on the energy level, more than likely the desire will not manifest in its expected form.

The higher self is only interested in the progress and survival of the soul or spirit. As far as it is concerned, everything else is just an arbitrary distraction from its true destiny. However, in order to keep you in balance and from going over the edge, the higher self allows for certain material preoccupations. This is why there will be times when your magic seems to work almost immediately, while on other occasions nothing happens. Results are dependent on the acquisition of energy from the higher

---

[1] The higher self is that part of the individual which is endowed with the urge to create, endowed with the urge to return to the perfection from which it came. It is the source of wisdom and knowledge and the divine spark within all individuals.

self to the lower self. The physical consciousness then changes this energy into usable power. This power can then be directed or focused towards the desired goal. All of this causes the reality of the objective to bend or move in accordance with will.

> *Mental energy is power; power supplies the force to bend reality.*

The entire purpose of magic is to create or cause a change. The key word here is *create*. In order for you to create or change something you must take action. Desire is not enough unless it is followed through on both the material as well as spiritual plane. Wishful thinking never changed anything, but action (work) does.

When all is said and done, magic is the most marvelous tool we have at our disposal. It permits us to create or reshape our own personal segment of the universe. Magic, when properly used, allows us the freedom to express our highest aspirations. For within the bounds of ritual magic the individual reigns supreme.

> *Magic is the tool we use to express our individual creativity in order to change our own personal reality.*

CHAPTER TWO

The Language of Magic

The Application of Elemental Energy

Every society, philosophy, or religion has its own unique language which expresses its purpose. Magic, as a reasoned doctrine, is no different. It has very distinctive symbols, methods of operation, and fundamental principles which communicate its objective. Once you have an understanding of this special language, magic automatically begins to work for you.

The language of magic is a symbolic one; intuitively understood within rather than verbalized. It is a language which takes us back to the beginning of time, when humankind's ability to create was expressed through its symbols. Symbols were (and still are) essential to our thinking. They add quality and meaning to that which surrounds us. Symbols are the fabric from which we form a fundamental understanding of life and our relationship to the universe.

Silently, yet profoundly, symbols speak to the spirit, intellect and emotions, creating an everlasting impression. It is through the integration of symbols and abstract concepts that we tap into the cosmic consciousness. This awareness of the universe brings us into alignment with the Divine or "All." [1] In time, this awareness arouses personal creativity, the divine spark within, and allows us to reclaim our personal power.

Mother Nature provides us with an abundance of rich and diverse symbolism. She instinctively stimulates our imaginations to produce original and productive ideas. Because humans have this ability to be individually creative, we, as a society, have been able to progress far beyond our ancestors' wildest dreams. Practitioners of the magical arts have long realized the importance of symbols and their ability to connect one form of consciousness to another. It is through the use of workable symbols, combined with focused energy, that the magician finds his or her greatest source of power.

Symbols surround us and speak to our minds without words. The red octagon-shaped sign at the end of the road tells us to stop; the green arrow on the light tells us to go. The cigarette in a circle with a line across its face tells us smoking is not allowed, while a simple drawing of a man or woman on a door indicates the intended gender occupancy of a bathroom.

Similarly, magic and ritual both use symbols to speak to our higher consciousness and enable us to act without effort to process information. This is a crucial concept, for *it is during the conversion process that energy and power are at their peak.* The time between absorption and transformation is when projection of desire occurs, and this must be accurate and spontaneous. There can be no break or interruption in the flow of focused energy.

In order for your higher self to be creative, it must be allowed to have interference-free space. One of the few times the higher self is allowed this special moment is dur-

---

[1] The "All" is the only source of intelligence and energy in one total construct. It is the source of all light, life, and energy, the Supreme Being, the Force.

ing a ritual. Then the conscious mind is distracted and inner dialogue is quieted, activating an automatic response mechanism. When actions become mechanical and instinctive, the higher self is allowed its all-important freedom to create, instead of just manipulating what already exists.

Symbols represent actions, desires, and results to the higher self and the conscious physical mind. When we allow a symbol to take over and represent an idea, our conscious mind is expanded. This outside stimulation blocks the processing procedure, thereby converting ordinary animation into creative energy. This creative energy is our divine spark, which can be focused and directed by the lower conscious to bring about a tangible demonstration of desire.

The value of this particular flash period is a realization of harmony, when the mind and body are able to react in accordance with will. Everything flows smoothly from the higher consciousness, through the mind, and out into the physical plane without interruption. The entire being is in perfect balance. Nothing is standing in its way or stopping it from being creative.

Symbols Evoke Creative Response

All symbols have power and in some way connect us to that which they represent. In turn, the energy we force through this connection will affect what resides on the opposite end. A good example of this would be blowing through a straw. Whatever is in the path of the air flow will be forced to move. Energy always affects or changes that with which it comes into contact.

In magic, the symbol we use to represent our request

acts like the straw. It directs personal energy towards a goal. What actually happens is our higher consciousness is being projected through the symbolic object, which then changes it to determine the final objective or result. Symbols are the connective link between the mundane consciousness, the creative spirit, and the manifestation of desire.

Symbols which evoke an emotional, mental or physical response have power. It is this power which is then focused and directed towards a goal. The idea is to manifest symbolic or mental images onto the material plane.

> *That which evokes a response has power.*

Ritual magic, unlike other philosophies or forms of positive thinking, incorporates the use of physical symbols and tools in its practice. Without effort, these implements help us reach other planes of consciousness. These symbols and tools enhance or extend individual personal power beyond the scope of corporeal identity. Just as the artist uses paints, brush and a canvas to bring his or her impressions into reality, so too will the magician use tools (symbolic tools) to help create or materialize his or her thoughts.

The Elements as Symbols

Within the bounds of ritual magic there are certain symbols for which everyone has an affinity. They are the basic constituents and foundation of all magical works and are at the core of physical life, resonating on a level of universal acceptance. It is this partiality to identical substance that creates a magical link between all living organisms, allowing for cause and effect. These primary symbols are in actuality elements which respond to both physical and mental sanction.

On the physical plane we see these elements as *air, fire, water and earth.* Symbolically they represent the intellect, determination or drive, feelings or emotions, creation and formulation. They give us the ability to reproduce in physical form what we mentally desire. These four elements are facts of life and come to us as fresh air, energy from the sun, water to drink, and the food which is provided by the earth. From a symbolic standpoint they represent qualities and conditions which we need to observe in order to align ourselves with the natural universe.

It is crucial in the practice of magic to have a thorough knowledge and understanding of these basic elements. Natural magic always seeks the avenue of least resistance, which is represented by the middle path of equilibrium. This middle path enables the mind and body to work in unison, which then provides a direct channel from which the creative energies can flow. Once the individual begins to work with the elemental energies, he or she once again becomes attuned to the delicate rhythms of nature. Then, and only then, is he or she able to manipulate the subtle forces of the universe.

The Element of Air

Air is symbolically related to breath. Air is thought to be a subtle material realm between the physical and spiritual plane. Air speaks to the intellect and brings forth the true essence of the individual through the creative imagination. The element of air in magic represents new beginnings, the thought process, and creativity.

Symbolically air is blue, relates to the East, and is expressed through the circle. It is represented by the Star card in the Tarot and astrologically equated with the sign of Aquarius.

The Element of Fire

Fire represents transformation, the life-giving generative powers of the sun. It is emblematic of a deity in many cultures. It is the element of fervent intensity, aspiration, and personal power. Fire is the force which motivates and drives all living organisms. Fire, along with air, creates energy, gets us going and produces stamina. "What the mind can imagine (air), the will (fire) can create."

Symbolically fire is red, relates to the South, and is expressed through a triangle. It is identified with the Strength card of the Tarot and astrologically is seen as Leo.

The Element of Water

The third basic element and the most primary form in which liquid can exist is feminine, passive and receptive. Water has long been seen as the source of all potentialities in existence. It is associated with the Great Mother, the universal womb, birth, and fertility. Water is emblematic of the life-giving and life-destroying ability of the cosmos. Water is used to cleanse or purify physically as well as psychically.

If air is the intellect, fire the energy or drive, then water becomes the emotional response to magical operations. The mysteries are formed, nurtured and given birth through the element of water. Water is like the Great Mother. When heated by the fire of passion, life is brought forth. But when cooled by the midnight air, silence and death are eminent. This is why so many religions use immersion in water to symbolize the return to a primordial state of purity. In essence, the baptism or dunking of an individual in water signifies death and rebirth of both the body and the spirit.

Magically, water is represented by the color green, a crescent moon, and the West. It is expressed through the Death card in the Tarot and astrologically equated with the sign of Scorpio.

The Element of Earth

Earth has the vibrational frequency which forms a solid quality. It is considered to be feminine in nature, passive and negative in polarity. The earth symbolically represents both the womb and the grave, that which brings life forth and that which takes it away or reclaims it. Unlike water, the earth is stationary and does not actively create. Earth is seen magically as the final outcome. It provides the other three elements with a place to physically manifest a desire. Earth is our base of operation, where we exhibit the final product of our imagination.

Earth is considered to be yellow or brown in color, relates to the North and is expressed through a square. It is represented by the Hierophant in the Tarot and astrologically equated with the sign of Taurus.

The Element of Creative Consciousness, the Spirit

The fifth element is, in actuality, the first of magical consideration. It functions within all existence and is the total animation and experience of creation.

Spirit is the indestructible life force within each and every atom: the absolute energy which motivates the universe. It is totally neutral and in complete harmony with its surroundings. Before, during, and after physical life, the spirit represents our individual as well as collective perception, that which we conceive, project and create. The spirit is the intelligent force which resides inside and outside of matter. It is entwined with the soul consciousness and is always good and correct.

In magic, the spirit is represented by a black oval, the void, or that which has no beginning or end. The spirit is an abstract perception and difficult to equate with physical symbols. The closest is the Fool card in the Tarot, which is seen as the scintillation of the intelligence which controls life. The Fool is insight, wisdom and folly, something unfinished, always reborn.

The spirit or soul can be seen as the connecting force which binds or unites all of the other elements together. This is best illustrated in the pentagram, where the four physical elements are all joined by crisscross lines, leading upwards towards their point of origin. Expressed here in a comprehensive form, we see the individual's higher consciousness or spirit totally centered or balanced, neutral and in a position of authority over his or her mundane desires. Meditation upon the pentagram will help bring us closer to the realization of inner harmony.

It is important to note that when we come into alignment with a symbol or an element through natural reflection, an affinity for its representation begins. What this means is, we begin to have an appreciation for, and understanding of, the image. This in turn gives us a certain amount of power and control over the element or symbol, and over that aspect of our personality or environment which the symbol represents.

Living With the Elements

Each element relates to a physical quality as well as a mental one. To really get to know the elements, it is necessary to feel them, work with them and use them in daily life. By incorporating these four natural elements into our daily routine, we actually begin to live magic rather than just observe it. This is important, as magic (or any philosophy) is useless if it cannot be applied to life and bring about desired results. Without a certain amount of obvious reward our consciousness becomes frustrated, energy levels drop and personal creative resources become depleted. This frustration is good when it inspires and forces action, but when it can't be satisfied it creates obsession or apathy.

Experience is always the best teacher. The following exercises will provide you with the experiences necessary to integrate the elements into daily life. It is the use of these subtle forces of the elements which help us align our consciousness to that of the cosmic order. This in turn develops our self-control, giving us power over our mundane nature.

For these exercises you will need to choose a symbol to represent each element. This can be something for which you already have an affinity, or you may pick one from the chart at the end of this chapter. Either way, the symbol with which you will be working should be one which represents the true nature of the element. The idea here is to have a physical representation of the symbol with which you are working, something you can hold or look at. This is important, because later on you will be learning how to transfer energy from you into physical objects, creating personal links for magical works.

EXERCISE ONE: *Working With Air*

Sit quietly and relax, as you do in your general meditation exercise. Hold your air object in your hand; look at it. Use your breath to control your thoughts. Breathe in to a count of five and then exhale to a count of five. Do this several times until your concentration is fixed upon the object. Feel the object become light, so light it could float. Because you are holding it, you too are so light you can float.

Feel yourself floating upward toward the blue sky, so lightly you drift like a feather in the wind. Feel the sun and fresh air upon your face as you float higher and higher, upward into the clear blue sky. As you soar above the ground, feel yourself being totally free and able to do anything you wish.

While you are in this state look around; what do you see? How do you feel? What thoughts present themselves? Keep floating, feeling free and able to do as you wish. It is during this time that original ideas will come to you. Remember these ideas. They represent your higher consciousness and its creative ability. The thoughts and ideas that present themselves during your contact with the air element are what you should be working on. These are the things that you, the real you, wants to do, create and complete. Take them with you as you begin to descend.

Slowly float downward until your feet touch the earth and you begin to feel the weight of your body. You are now in total touch with reality and have the knowledge of your air journey to help guide you toward your desired goal.

EXERCISE TWO: *Working With Fire*

Sit quietly, relax, and use your breath (to the count of five) to control your thoughts as before. Holding or looking at the fire symbol, feel yourself growing hot; feel the heat and energy of the fire element flow through your body. Feel yourself being totally engulfed in flames, yet not being harmed in any way. You are all powerful, you have the energy and ability to accomplish anything you wish. You are strong, forceful, and filled with energy.

Point your fingers and see the flames shoot from their tips. See these flames turn into energy and power;

power that allows you to move things without touching them. See the pure energy of life being projected from the tips of your fingers.

Now, taking the ideas that were given to you during your air journey, see yourself doing these things. Make things happen through your own personal power and energy. You are as the flame—hot and powerful, and you can do what you set out to do. You burn with passion and power and the will to accomplish your goals. Allow this impression of your ability to achieve to be burned into your consciousness.

Slowly feel the warmth begin to cool. Slowly come back to reality, while still retaining that sense of personal power, that knowledge of your ability to make manifest your desires.

EXERCISE THREE: *Working With Water*

Relax and use your breath to control your thoughts. Holding or looking at your water symbol, begin to feel cool, clear, fresh water surrounding you. You are floating on top of the waves. It is restful, quiet, and you can see the clear blue sky overhead.

Slowly, allow the water to cover you; begin to sink beneath the surface of the water until you are completely immersed in it. Do not be afraid. Like a fish you are completely at home. Swim around under the surface of the water. See the other fish, plants and underwater growth. Feel how calm and quiet everything is. You are totally aware of everything around you, and yet nothing can harm you or disturb the sense of peace you feel. The water is absorbing your problems, your negative thoughts, and giving you a feeling of deep emotional security.

You know that no matter what happens to you, the water will be there to help restore your vitality. It will provide you with the rest you need to help regenerate and re-organize your thoughts. This is a time of total quiet when you can really reach deep inside and feel your total being. A time to learn how your emotions react, a time to get in touch with the real you. When in the water, you are safe from the outside world so you can take the time to just be.

Slowly float to the surface. See the sky above as you begin to get out of the water; feel the warmth of the sun and the cool breeze of the air as it refreshes you. Be sure to remember how you felt while you were in the water. Take this feeling of being totally, (psychically and emotionally) clean and refreshed with you. Know that when you begin to get emotional about something you can wash this feeling away with the water element. This will help allow you to see things as they really are when not clouded by negative emotions.

EXERCISE FOUR: *Working With Earth*

As before, relax and use your breath to control your thoughts. Hold and look at your earth symbol. Visualize a cave set deep within the earth. Now enter the cave, allowing your eyes to adjust to the dark. Then proceed to go deeper and deeper into the cave. Downward, spiraling downward, ever deeper into the cave.

Hear the trickle of the underwater stream which travels through the cave. Look at the cave walls. What do you see? How do you feel as you go deeper and deeper into the cave? What impressions about yourself do you get that are connected with your being in the cave?

Look up and see a tiny slit, far above; see the shaft of light coming through to light the way, revealing the inner depths of the cave. Look and see the crystals and different shaped rocks, the pale green moss that carpets the floor, everything has such beauty and elegance, the kind of beauty that only Mother Nature creates.

Breathe deeply, feel the heavy, earth-scented air enter your body, giving you a strength and vitality that you haven't had before. Feel the cave floor beneath you. Pick up a handful of the dark moist earth; look at it, feel it, smell it, absorb its richness. Feel your connection to the earth and know you are part of it. Allow the life-giving qualities of the earth to penetrate you, giving you strength and reassurance in your own abilities.

Be still, reflect on the cave and the total protection it provides. Now slowly begin your journey back. Before leaving say a little prayer to the Earth Mother. Thank her for this time of solitude and companionship and take the security of the earth energy with you.

These exercises should help you to see and appreciate the revitalizing powers of the elements. They should provide you with a sense of knowledge and aid you in tapping into this great reservoir of elemental energy. You should begin to feel and use their life-giving properties to help create and achieve what you most desire.

It is a good idea to pick a symbol for each element and stick with it. This continuity will help create a link between the actual physical object and your consciousness. In time you will only need to hold your symbol to recreate these feelings of alignment. Just the physical contact alone will help to ground and center you in a moment of stress. This will provide you with that all important edge, the ability to regroup your thoughts and act accordingly out of knowledge, rather than emotion.

CHAPTER THREE

The Symbolic Ritual Tools

The Elemental Weapons of Magic

The next phase in learning the art of magic involves understanding the relationship between symbolism and physical objects. It is necessary to realize the connection between images, symbols and elements in association with the thought and creation process. This is important, because it is through physical symbols that we are able to focus our attention and energy.

Symbols are tools which become representations of our ability to project our consciousness. We all use tools in some fashion or another to help accomplish the tasks placed before us. Just as every commonplace profession has specific symbols or tools which make a statement about its purpose, so do the magical arts. The only real difference is most of the tools used in magic are of a symbolic nature, rather than of actual functional design.

Symbolic tools have a two-fold objective. First, they elicit an automatic reaction. Second, they channel creative energy toward a specific goal. It is this drawing from within and then projecting outward which allows us to manifest our desires. No matter what anyone says to the contrary, tools (or props) are vital to the practice of magic.

There are those who do not agree with the use of tools and loudly proclaim it is the mind and only the mind (thinking) which brings about results. Were this true everyone would be thinking themselves into the White House, or the Taj Mahal—or projecting their svelte bodies onto the beaches on the Riviera. So, there must be some link or contributing factor between aspiration and manifestation. Something which produces the connection or contact point between imagination and final reward.

What will help bring our wishes into reality? What is the missing link between thinking and acquiring? What allows some people to get what they want, when others, no matter how hard they try, never seem to succeed? The answer is simple. You must know how to use the tools of your trade. A carpenter cannot build a house if he doesn't know which end of the hammer to use. A computer is of little use if you can't figure out how to turn it on. Tools go hand in hand with knowledge, experience and accomplishment, no matter what the trade.

In order to make things happen the way we want them to, we must know how to properly use the symbolic representations of physical-plane images. We must be able to effectively relate to and utilize the symbols and tools which represent our intention and request. This means we must learn to use material plane phenomena in combination with positive thinking. For it is the combination of mental thought forms and physical action which creates the dynamic energy needed to make things happen. It is dynamic energy which allows us to take intangible thoughts or dreams and make them real.

> ### Dynamic energy is a product of the mind in conjunction with the emotions.

Through the use of magic, *fantasy becomes fact.* We are able to externalize the dream or desire by the use of proper symbolic imagery. This is accomplished when we pull down the seed of creation from our higher consciousness and force it to physically manifest on the material plane. Tools and symbols are the most expedient and efficient way to make this happen.

In the practice of magic there are five major symbolic tools which represent the forces and expressions of life. A complete explanation of each tool follows this quick reference chart.

Wand	Sword	Chalice	Pentacle	Mirror
air	fire	water	earth	spirit
intellect	ambition	emotion	expression	creator
spring	winter	summer	fall	timeless
birth	life	death	regeneration	eternity
ideas	action	nurturing	manifestation	intuition
blue	red	green	yellow	black
circle	triangle	crescent	square	oval

THE WAND, ROD, OR STAFF: The wand is ideally suited for directing personal power. Its phallic, tubular shape allows your intellectual-psychic energy to be channeled towards a desired objective. By virtue of its shape alone it is masculine in nature. During ritual, the wand becomes an extension of the individual using it. Personal power is then forced with a laser-like intensity toward the desired goal. The wand is the tool of creation; through it the seeds of desire are allowed to manifest. In all of magic, myth and legend, wands have always been able to bring into reality what the individual wishes. The magician and his/her wand are inseparable because together they represent the very essence of change. This is in accordance with the will of the combined ability of humankind and the cosmos to manifest desire.

There is a great deal of dispute over whether the wand should be connected with air or fire. From my point of view, and for magical reasons, the wand is strictly an instrument of the air element. This is one reason our ancestors made their wands from young tree branches. The fresh growth was not only indicative of spring and the seasons to come, but represented the concept of new beginnings. An important point to note here is, "Time honored tradition contains power." The entire process of first cause, inception, origination and progenitor are ingrained within the symbology of the wand, making it a tool of mind.

The element of air is intellect and it provides the environment where abstract thoughts originate. These thoughts enter our consciousness when our creative higher self initiates the manifestation process. This inner communication is one of the keys to magical success. No amount of wonderful ideas will do us any good if we cannot get them out and make them real. The single most important act in magic is personal dialogue, which produces the realization of desire. This is then coupled with the act of formulation to produce tangible results.

Both symbolically and physically the wand is best suited to the purpose of magical creation. This is how it works: you formulate an idea and then you bring it down into your active consciousness. Once you have a clear picture of what you want, you force all of your attention in that direction. This is done by projecting the flow of personal energy to a specific target area. The "target area" is a symbolic representation of the desired outcome, and the wand acts like a laser, directing the flow of power from you to its destination.

Even though this is all symbolic, it is none the less real. Thought is energy and takes up space. Therefore, it is only reasonable to assume that if you force another energy into an already occupied space what is there must move or change. This is what magic does best, change, move, or replace what is unwanted with what is desired. The wand assists with that process.

It is not unheard of for practitioners of the magical arts to have several different wands—one for healing, another for works of prosperity, even one for creating peace and love. Each is different, unique and special according to its particular intention. Wands are very versatile. The only physical requirement of the wand is that it should be rod-like and phallic in shape. Size, design and ornamentation become a matter of personal choice.

Wands are easy to make. Attaching a rock or crystal to a small branch that has been wrapped in leather works nicely. A simple copper tube with crystals, amethyst, or rose quartz connected to the ends produces a wonderful energy conductor. Brass tubing found in most craft shops has all sorts of possibilities, and even wooden dowels from a lumber store can, with some imagination, be turned into elegant wands.

My personal wand is made from copper tubing. It is eleven inches long and has a rose quartz on one end and an amethyst on the other. Silver solder spirals down the shaft, connecting the ends. On the shaft are four stones: garnet, rhodocrosite, gem silica, and lapis. Because of the magical properties associated with these particular gems, this combination helps to balance power through self-love and spiritual insight.

This is a picture of my copper wand. It has amethyst and rose quartz ends. Other stones are attached to the rod.

Whether you make or buy a wand, the decision is yours. There are many who will insist that all magical tools should be constructed by the individual using them. This is a wonderful sentiment for those who have the time, the equipment, and are artistically inclined. For some this is not only unrealistic but impossible. The most important consideration when making or choosing a magical tool is, how does it feel to you? Will this be something you can relate to and work with? Remember, in magic you are in control, you are the power, and you make all the decisions which affect your personal arena.

THE FIRE DAGGER, ATHAME, OR SWORD: In most traditional occultism, the sword or double-edged knife (athame or dagger), represents the element of fire and the masculine, positive force of nature. There is a good reason for this. Think about the process used to create a knife. Before the technology of iron smelting was known, knives were fashioned from flint. When the flint knife was rubbed with another piece of flint, it would produce a spark. Whether the knife was fashioned by hand with flint, or forged into shape from an iron smelting process, the element of fire was involved, leaving an indelible impression of its essential masculine quality upon the blade.

Fire has always been considered a representation of force, strength and will, and so has fire's symbolic tool, the sword. When we see someone use the sword, we are able to see in physical form just what power can do.

The ritual dagger or athame. This one is made of brass and was discovered in an antique shop.

The sword has played an important role in many legends and myths. Throughout history many myths have been written about the young hero who wields a magical weapon, coming to the rescue of lady, land and ideal. Probably the best known is Excalibur, the mighty sword of King Arthur given him by the Lady of the Lake. As long as Arthur was in possession of the sword he was invincible. Truth or fiction, it matters not; the symbology of the sword remains the only consideration.

Swords come in all shapes, sizes and designs. In the West we see them as being straight and phallic in shape. To the practitioner of the East, swords are curved and feminine in their appearance. This is due to their legends depicting women as being powerful because of their hold over the life processes. However, for our purpose the sword will remain as our Western legends have conditioned us to perceive it, straight and phallic in expression.

Swords, like wands, are used for directing personal power. They help focus energy in a desired direction for a specific purpose. This is their function, to help regulate as well as conduct the flow of internal expression toward a desired destination.

With so much emphasis placed on tools in the practice of magic, it becomes imperative to remember *it is not the objects themselves which are of great consequence, but rather what they represent*. Tools are only symbols and they serve to direct energy toward a desired goal.

THE CHALICE, CUP, OR CAULDRON: In order to fully appreciate and avail ourselves of the benefit of the water element, it must first be confined or contained within a suitable vessel. For most magical practices, the chalice, cup, or cauldron serves in this capacity to represent the feminine, watery side of nature. The chalice is totally feminine in its nature.

Ocean tides and the fluid, liquid, watery realms of our beginnings push and pull us into sympathetic response with our surroundings. For it is this feminine reverberation, or emotional union with nature, which causes us to react. Properly embraced, emotions keep us in balance. However, unbridled passion will create havoc and dissipate energy.

As with the sword, there have been countless stories told about beautiful chalices and magical cauldrons: Arthur and his knights in search of the Grail, the Cauldron of Cerridwen with its regenerative powers, and of course the Witches of Macbeth stirring the cauldron with their bubbling brew of sordid ingredients. These tales serve as examples of how we try to dominate and to bring into reality the substance of emotional consciousness.

There is very little, if any, dispute over the symbolic representation of the chalice or cauldron. Its design is

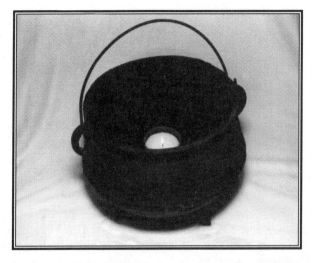

This is our cauldron, in which we always keep a candle burning. It represents the eternal flame and the fire of life. The only time it is allowed to go out is before Yule and then it is relit in celebration of the rebirth of the sun/son.

The chalice or sacred cup. This one is made of brass and brass and is pictured here resting on the brass plate used for cakes during ritual. When not in use, the chalice is kept covered.

emblematic of the womb, the Mother Goddess, and the ability to regenerate. This probably accounts for its presence in so many ancient Egyptian, Babylonian and even Christian temples, as it was through the process of spiritual rebirth that an individual gained wisdom, inspiration and enlightenment.

Another aspect to the water element and its corresponding symbolic imagery is the challenge or quest factor. Seeking to discover the hidden mysteries of life and death, early humans took to the sea. Thinking the earth flat, they thought they would surely drop off into the great void were they to sail far enough. How astonished they must have been when they found others like themselves, rather than the edge of the universe which they feared. But the quest itself to find and touch their creator far outweighed their fear of death.

This is how a chalice, like the Grail, fits into magic. It contains the mystery, the hope, and promise of that which is attained when all has been set to rest. It is open to observation, yet only the surface of what it contains can be seen. One needs to delve deeply within to truly discover what secrets it holds. The emotional factor of that which is yet unknown will in itself create a powerful energy flow.

THE DISK OR SHIELD: The disk (or shield) is not so much a tool as it is the representation of humankind's ability to create or manifest an idea. Magicians use the symbol of the disk to conceptualize their thoughts, believing that what they see in their mind's eye they will surely realize in physical form. The disk becomes the point of focus, much like the center of a stage during a play, where all the magician's attention is directed. It is this momentary address of energy towards a single purpose that brings results.

Much like the cup or chalice, the disk represents the renewal or regeneration of life and is feminine in its nature. However, the disk is a more brooding, generative, dualistic symbol because it is both protective and death-dealing. This is brought out clearly in many of the old myths and legends. We see the Knights of the Round Table with their shields (representing their family, life ties) as they go into battle. The shield would protect them from the death-dealing blows of their adversaries, while at the same time allowing them to strike back and possibly kill their foe.

The Pentacle. This one is made of wood, and represents the earth and the ability of the higher self to control the ever-present elements of nature.

From the spiritual and esoteric view, we see the disk as a symbol of unity. The sun disk with crescent horns represents the sacred marriage of the Divine Pair. The round shape of the disk represents both the earth and the womb. The carvings or etchings on its face will be of a masculine nature. Together these convey the masculine and feminine energy, conjoined for the purpose of creation. This is why we need tools, to help us balance our (feminine) thoughts with (masculine) energy, thus allowing for creation process to take place.

The beauty of the disk is its versatility. It provides the practitioner of magic with a mode of expression, like the canvas for an artist. You can place any number of unique, symbolic designs on the face of the disk or shield. This will represent, to your higher consciousness, an idea in picture form of what you wish to achieve.

An example would be placing the logo of a magical order upon the face of the disk, then using that disk in ritual. All of the energy which was raised and then focused towards the disk would be going for the good of the group as a whole. This is how symbols help us achieve what we want. They force personal power to go in a specific direction rather than allowing it to scatter and dissipate. The more you use the tool, the more distinctive and focused the energy becomes. By directing our thoughts through the wand and onto the disk we refine our energy to a considerable extent.

THE MIRROR: The mirror represents wisdom, the mind, higher self and the soul: "The mirror of the universe." It is the reflection of the supernatural and divine intelligence. The mirror is seen as a gateway between the worlds and also humankind's knowledge of itself. Mirrors are used as doors to the astral planes and for transmitting and receiving communications. For the most part, mirror working is reserved for higher initiates and those with a good deal of ritual experience. As the rituals presented in this book do not require the presence of a mirror I have limited my comments about it.

— CHAPTER FOUR —

The Definition of Ritual

Its Structure and Purpose

This book, or any other for that matter, is worth little if you are not willing to apply its knowledge to your present situation. Pure and simple, we are all physical beings attached to a material world. If we want to be successful, we must react to our environment in a rational manner, mainly because logic values the system in which it retains its own momentum. Magic, through the use of imaginary, symbolic tools, and ritual, helps the individual realign with the natural forces and energies of the universe. In return, this alignment will bring about change, growth, progress and inner harmony.

"What the mind can imagine, the will can create" should be every aspiring magician's motto. The only thing standing in your way or keeping you from getting what you want is your inability to manifest your thoughts. However, this can be changed through the use of magic and proper ritual procedure.

Just What is a Ritual?

A ritual is a prescribed event or particular ceremony that is built up by tradition and carries with it a great amount of energy, light, force and impact. Atmosphere, dress and symbology contribute to the event, as does the use of repetitious activity. The key to effective ritual is repetitious activity. By this I mean doing the exact same thing, in the exact same way, each and every time. This one single point cannot be stressed enough. Spontaneous ritual is fun, but repetitious ritual is effective.

What is Ritual Magic?

Ritual magic is the creation of a specific ceremony (using repetitious activity in a controlled environment) to create or force a change to occur in accordance with your will. The only reason for doing ritual magic is to change something, even if the change is only one of personal attitude.

Everything is in a constant state of change and as we are part and party to the universal consciousness, we must learn to go with the flow or be swept away by its momentum. If you are going to do magic, you must be willing to accept the unavoidable process of change. It is only when you change your attitude, outlook, and way of thinking that things around you begin to change as well.

Change can be very frightening to the poor ego. (The ego is the conditioned, motivating force which was formed outside of our own determined will; it is that which projects, protects, and receives information for the true identity or soul essence of the individual. It is the mask you wear for others to see.) The ego's fear of change often surfaces when one begins to dabble in the magical arts. Once the higher self begins to see the possibilities which lie before it, it will no longer tolerate excuses as to why it doesn't have what it needs and wants. This is something to consider before you get involved. The higher self will tolerate ignorance but not laziness.

The main reason for doing magic is to help you get what you want. This is accomplished through specific ceremonies and rituals designed to distract the ego or conscious self. These distractions allow the higher self the time and space it needs to create or bring into being a projected desire. The opportunity for the higher self to express itself is not enough. It also needs a certain amount of justification for its actions. There has to be an inner understanding of what is actually taking place and why. The higher self accepts logic and facts, not fantasy and delusion. When the facts are properly presented through ritual, the higher self reacts and produces results. All magic works when properly executed. It is only a matter of distracting the lower self, or ego, long enough for the higher self to be able to get something accomplished. This is done by occupying the childish ego with all sorts of trinkets and things to do. During this time, the higher self is able to sneak off and create something of value. This is why tools, symbols, and atmosphere are so important. You must totally occupy the lower self, or doubting ego, in order for the higher self to have the freedom and space to produce desirable results.

The easiest and most efficient way to enter into ritual magic is by becoming aware of the natural forces which surround us. By aligning ourselves with natural forces, becoming aware of cycles and changes in our environment, we begin to flow with the universe. Once we are caught up in this current of universal movement, it is only natural to feel its power. We begin to feel connected to, rather than separated from, that which surrounds us.

It is imperative, for magical purposes, to be able to relate to our surroundings. We must be able to feel the energy flowing through us, combining our individual power with that which already exists. It is only reasonable to take advantage of what is here and now, as this simplifies the entire creation process, and speeds up the time involved in manifesting a desire.

Three Reasons for Doing Ritual:

(1) SPIRITUAL—to spiritually align oneself with a specific divine energy source, such as an Archangel.
(2) RELIGIOUS—to celebrate a specific day or time of power i.e., Full Moons, Sabbats, beginning of the year, etc.
(3) MATERIAL—to create or manifest a desired goal for the purpose of obtaining something on the material plane. This could be anything from getting a raise in pay to healing a consenting injured friend.

It is important that your motives or intentions are clear for they will greatly influence your productivity during ritual. The higher self knows why you are doing something. Be honest with yourself. Your reasons are your own and perfectly justifiable if approached in a sincere manner. The point of doing any ritual is to create a flow of energy, not engage in battle with your higher consciousness.

The Four Parts to Every Ritual

Once you have considered the reason for doing a ritual and decided upon a theme, you need to construct the ceremony itself. When preparing any ritual there are four distinct segments with which you must deal if the ritual is to be effective. All four of these segments must combine effortlessly in order for the ritual to flow smoothly.

1. The first segment is the *preparation and consecration*. This is important, as it sets the tone of the ritual and the mood.

In this first part, we will consider the physical setting of the ritual area. Make a list all of the items that will be needed and note their proper position. While you are setting up, you will actually be creating sacred space. This is done by the consecrating and casting of the magic circle, the creating of a boundary line of energy. This is the actual beginning of the ceremony, and should be in writing so there is no mistake as to what needs to be done. In time, this entire procedure should be memorized and become second nature to the practitioner.

It is during this time, after the circle has been set, that the invocations to the God and Goddess are done. The invocations draw the special essence of the deity with which you are working down into the participant in order to bless and empower the work.

2. The next step in the ritual procedure is that of *the petition*. The petition describes in some form or another the reason for doing the ritual. It may be a story, a descriptive poem or just a simple prayer to a special deity. The most important aspect of the petition is the statement of the petitioner's desire. During this segment of the ritual, chanting is used to raise energy for the petition. Chanting is the toning of a chosen sound or rhythmic poem to accomplish a definite purpose. Chants are repetitive and are usually spoken in a monotone, with varying degrees of intensity. To start the chant, members take hands and pass energy from one person to the next around the circle. The rhythm of the chant and the intensity causes the energy level within both the individuals and the circle itself to rise. This energy is then directed to towards the desired goal.

3. The third segment of the ritual is *the sacrifice*. This is the period of time when symbolic offerings are made. These offerings are usually made to enhance the consideration of our ritual petitions, or are remembrances of something

special we received. This is also the section of the ritual when the Blessing of the Cakes and Wine or the Rite of Union is performed. The Rite of Union is the part of the ceremony where the true masculine and feminine energy of the universe is conjoined, thereby energizing sacred fluid from which all may partake.

4. The last part of the ceremony is *the banishment or closing*. At this time, the ceremony is brought to an end and all of the energies raised in the circle are banished. This is important because raised energy needs to be let go in order to be able to work. Another reason for getting rid of the raised energy is that you don't want it to interfere with other projects which may be at cross purpose to each other.

Whenever you write a ritual, it is a good idea to keep the above instructions in mind. These suggestions will help you format your ceremonies in an organized manner so they will present a clear purpose and flow smoothly.

The Ritual Check List

Next to be considered is the ritual check list. This should express in written form the totality of your intent, as well as what you will need to bring it about.

• *Define your desire and intent.* What is it you want? For what reason are you going to do a ritual? Be honest, because this will add drive and energy to your work.

• *Categorize the objective.* Into what category does your desire fall? Are you doing something for a spiritual reason, such as celebrating some special time of power such as the full moon; or is there something that you wish or need? Don't be afraid to write down what you want. If you are too embarrassed to put your desires into writing because you feel they are unworthy, then you should not attempt to bring them into manifestation. This will cause you to be at cross-purposes with your higher self and in the long run will not make you happy.

• *Construct the ritual.* Once you have carefully considered your desire and the category into which it falls, you will need to align yourself with the proper forces. This is accomplished through the symbolism, tools, time and place of the ritual.

A ritual is like a play because it expresses an idea or concept in material form. This makes an impression on both the surrounding atmosphere and the consciousness of the individual(s) involved. You might consider this to be a great game of pretend, where you coerce yourself into believing that what you most desire is taking place. In reality, you are forcing your intentions on the environment which creates a space for the desire, enabling it to exist.

• *Prepare yourself for the ritual.* A personal time of meditation and contemplation prior to ritual is essential. You should always take at least an hour to an hour and a half to prepare yourself for any ceremony. Just the day-to-day rush and vibrational energy which surrounds us needs to be balanced out to effectively function in ritual.

The best way to begin any ceremony or ritual is with a cleansing bath. This will help get rid of any negativity to which you might have been exposed during the course of the day. Besides being relaxing, bath time allows us a chance for personal introspection and meditation upon what we need and want.

A part of preparation that is often overlooked is set-up time. This is when you dress, set up the altar, and prepare the room or area for the ceremony. Set-up time should always be considered part of the ritual itself. Remember, rituals are like plays in which we express a physical desire in symbolic form to our higher consciousness. As in any play, the props, stage setting, and choreography are an integral part of its effectiveness. Soft, ritualistic (New Age) music, the aroma of incense, and even a small glass of your favorite wine or herbal tea can help set the mood. This is important. You need to be totally relaxed and in the proper frame of mind before you start any ritual.

You have never seen actors start a play before the stage has been set, unless of course they are just rehearsing. Just as actors study their lines to rehearse for a play, you too should always read through a ritual several times before doing it. If there are others participating, there should be a rehearsal of the ritual. This will help avoid mistakes and allow everything to move smoothly.

Ritual should be enjoyable, not something that everyone does because they feel they have to. If you are going to do a ritual, do it correctly. And remember, a good ritual, properly constructed and performed, always works.

Rituals do not necessarily have to be elaborate or complicated to achieve their purpose. In fact, this is where so many make their greatest mistake. They attempt to enlist the power of every conceivable magical item and incantation known to man. What they end up with is something that resembles an auctioneer at a flea market rather than a practitioner of the magical arts. On the other hand, a ritual without the appropriate components, energy, and enthusiasm is just as useless.

Balance is the key to an effective ritual. It means knowing what, when, and where to use your magical tools and symbols so that they are most effective. You don't see a carpenter carrying every tool he owns to the top of the ladder just to nail in a single board. He surveys the job and takes up only what he needs. Ritual magic is no different. You should take time to plan exactly what you wish to accomplish and find the appropriate items you need for the ritual. You take only those tools and symbols needed into the ritual. Use common sense. You only want to distract the lower self, not confuse it to the point of stupefaction.

CHAPTER FIVE

For As Above, So Below

Choosing and Working With Deity

Since the beginning of time, humankind has looked to the heavens for inspiration. The sun became a God, the moon became a Goddess, and their children the stars filled the skies. Majestic mountains, winding rivers, underground caverns and towering trees became their dwelling places upon the earth. Their powers were awesome, their conquests are legend and their love for mankind is unquestionable. They have not died, they have not gone away, they are only waiting for you to bid them welcome—today.

While this book is not about religion, it does stress the presence of higher forces, those of a God and Goddess, within the framework of certain rituals. It is important for us to learn to connect with these forces, or Gods, because we have been separated from them for too long. In essence, we need to become friends with the Gods in order to share in their knowledge, wisdom and power.

Energy and Deity

Within the universe there are certain levels of conscious energy which have always existed. Our ancestors recognized these special forces and gave them individual identities and human characteristics. By doing this, they were able to relate to them on a more intimate and personal level. It was this relationship, with these constructs of conscious energy, that eventually produced the various pantheons of Gods and Goddesses which now exist.

Initially, it is necessary to understand the nature of these energy forces (or Gods) and what they can do for you. It is very simple. The relationship between an individual and God is very much like the relationship between that individual and his or her bank account. However, instead of dealing with a bank and money you are dealing with a *God form* and *energy*.

If you want to have a bank account, you need to choose a bank in which to put your money. Then, you open the account by identifying yourself and depositing money into it. At regular intervals you will put more money into the account. For your consideration of support, and the use of your money, the bank pays you interest. The more money you put into the bank account, the more interest you receive and the more money you end up with. It is the same thing with the God and Goddess. You find the pantheon of Gods you want to work with, then you invest your energy, rather than your money, into it.

The first step in choosing a pantheon of Gods and Goddesses, with which to work, is to familiarize yourself with them. This is best done by reading about the Gods and learning what types of energy they represent. The next step is to select a major God and Goddess from the pantheon who best represent, to you, the archetypal masculine and feminine forces of the universe. Once a rapport has been established with these two deities, you can proceed to learn about the other members of the pantheon[1].

The most important thing to remember when choosing a God and Goddess is to *choose the ones with which you feel comfortable.* Just because Joe up the street is working with Isis and Osiris doesn't necessarily mean you should work with them as well. If you feel more of an affinity towards Cerridwen and Cernunnos, then these are the ones you should choose. This is a personal choice based on your spiritual awareness and personal feelings of kinship with a certain pantheon. Only you know how you feel, and what will best serve your needs.

The following descriptions of Gods and Goddesses are from several different pantheons. These are by no means the only ones available to you and are offered only as suggestions. As you read through these descriptions, allow yourself time to think about each one of them individually, and ponder what they mean to you.

When you begin reading about the Gods, it is a good idea to make notes on how you feel about each one of them.[2] Which ones stir your emotions? Which ones do you instinctively feel affection towards? Which ones represent the concepts you are most interested in working with? Above all, which ones do you want to give your energy to, and become friends with? If you take the time to consider each of the Gods individually, it will make your final selection process much easier.

---

[1] In most cases the focus of minor deities is on the material aspects of life, i.e., money, love, and health, whereas the focus of your major archetypes is on dynamic energy and progressive spiritual growth.

[2] *The New Larousse Encyclopedia of Mythology* is an excellent source for information on the major pantheons of gods and goddesses.

The God and Goddess

CELTIC

The Goddess dominates much of the Celtic culture. Although there are many male deities, they usually take second place to the female deities, who represent the land and earth. The Goddess represents the life-giving and destroying aspects of nature. She is the maiden in spring, the mother in summer, the crone in fall and the great transformer in winter.

Cerridwen

Cerridwen is the Celtic Mother Goddess of the moon and grain. She is especially known for her fearsome death totem, a white corpse-eating Sow. Cerridwen is associated with Astarte or Demeter and her harvest celebrations express her ability to both give life and take it away.

Cerridwen is also known as the Goddess of inspiration and knowledge because of her inexhaustible cauldron[3] in which she brewed a magic draught called "greal." This draught would give inspiration and knowledge to any who drank of it.

Cerridwen's concepts are expressed clearly in the myth about Gwion Bach. According to the story, this young boy got some of the liquid from the cauldron on his finger. The liquid gave him knowledge. Because the liquid was meant for someone else, Cerridwen relentlessly and angrily pursued him in many disguises. When she caught up with him, he turned into a grain of wheat and she a hen. She swallowed the grain, giving birth to a male child nine

---

[3] This cauldron was called Amen. The cauldron is considered to be the symbol of life and death and regeneration. It is symbolic of the womb and its creation process.

months later. Immediately, Cerridwen set the baby adrift upon the river. He was later discovered and in time became the great bard, Taliesin.

Correspondences (Cerridwen)

Archetype:	Crone, initiator.
Expression:	Mother of inspiration.
Time:	Full moon, midnight.
Season:	Harvest (winter).
Objects:	Cauldron, cup.
Number:	Three (combinations of three).
Colors:	Green, blue-green, silver, or white.
Animals:	Sow, hen, greyhound, otter, hawk.
Trees:	Elder, yew.
Plants:	Corn, barley, hellebore, patchouli, ivy, morning glory, mimosa, belladonna.
Stones:	Moonstone, beryl, chalcedony.

Cernunnos

Cernunnos is the Celtic God of vegetation, fertility, and the Underworld. Cernunnos is the stag God, Lord of the Beasts and master of woodland animals. His name means "Horned One" and he is usually depicted with ram's horns and serpents. His horns are a symbol of strength, power, and virility. The snakes are phallic and symbolic of regeneration.

Cernunnos can be seen as part man and part beast. He is the one who guards the portals of the Underworld and ushers those seeking transformation into the mysteries. He is the giver of life and the bringer of death. Like most horned Gods, he is concerned with the earth and how human life parallels its rhythms and cycles. Of prime importance is the idea of growing and becoming strong to ensure the survival of life and the land.

Correspondences (Cernunnos)

Archetype:	Guardian, regenerator.
Expression:	Father of life .
Season:	Summer.
Time:	Noon day sun.
Objects:	Torc necklace, horns, cornucopia, stang.
Number:	Six.
Colors:	Red, orange, yellow, sometimes black or brown.
Animals:	Stag, ram, serpent, dog, eagle.
Tree:	Oak.
Plants:	Bay, benzoin, juniper, mistletoe, orange, sun flower, marigold.
Stones:	Agate, carnelian, jasper.

EGYPTIAN

Isis (Greek for Aset)

Isis, whose name means throne, is the personification of the Great Goddess in her aspect of maternal devotion. She is the daughter of Seb and Nut, wife and sister of Osiris, and mother to Horus. She is always represented as a woman and wears on her head the throne, which is also the hieroglyph for her name. However, at times her headdress is a solar disk with horns, or it can also be the vulture's cap.

Myth and legend confirm Isis as the true wife and mother. For when her husband Osiris was killed by his jealous brother, Set, she spared no pains in finding his hidden body. However, once she found it, Set recaptured it and cut it into fourteen pieces. He then scattered these pieces throughout the land. Isis hunted all the pieces down and magically reconstituted the body. She then made love with Osiris, conceived, and gave birth to Horus.

Isis was worshipped as "the great magic" who protected her son Horus from predators and other dangers. It was believed that because of this, she would protect mortal children from the perils of daily life as well.

Correspondences (Isis)

Archetype:	Mother, protectress.
Expression:	Mistress of magic.
Time:	New moon.
Season:	Spring or Summer.
Objects:	Thet (knot or buckle), scepter, cup, horns, mirror.
Number:	Two or eight.
Colors:	Sky blue, green, gold, white.
Animals:	Snake, goose, owl, hawk, ram.
Trees:	Fig, willow.
Plants:	Lotus, lily, narcissus, myrtle, myrrh, iris, date-palm.
Stones:	Lapis, aquamarine, sapphire.

Osiris

Osiris symbolizes the divine in mortal form. He is the personification of physical creation and its cycles of birth, life, death and return. He is the highest of all powers, the King who brought civilization to the land of Egypt. He is husband and brother to Isis, father of Horus, and son of Seb and Nut.

Osiris was treacherously murdered by his brother Set who was considered to be the power of evil and darkness. After his death and resurrection, Osiris became the lord of the Underworld and the judge of the dead. He presides in the seat of judgment, when the heart of the deceased is weighed against the feather of Ma-at, and Thoth records the verdict.

Osiris is usually portrayed as a mummified, bearded man wearing the white crown of the North. Around his neck is an elaborate pectoral necklace and the menat counterpoise. He carries the shepherd's crook, the symbol of sovereignty and responsibility, and the flail that separates the wheat from the chaff.

Correspondences (Osiris)

Archetype:	King, priest.
Expression:	Father of stability and growth.
Time:	Setting sun.
Seasons:	Fall and winter
Objects:	Djed, crook, flail, menat, *was* (scepter).
Numbers:	Seven, fourteen, and twenty-eight.
Colors:	Gold, yellow, green, and white.
Animals:	Hawk, jackal, ape, bull.
Trees:	Cypress, thorn.
Plants:	Acacia, ivy, papyrus, orris, lily, storax, bay, frankincense, dittany.
Stones:	Topaz, quartz crystal, carnelian.

ASSYRO-BABYLONIAN

Ishtar

In Babylonian scripture, Ishtar was called the "Light of the World, Leader of Hosts and Opener of the Womb." She was also the "Lady of Battles" and considered to be valiant among the Goddesses. She was the "Goddess of the morn and Goddess of the evening" and the divine personification of the planet Venus.

Sacred prostitution was an integral part of her cult. When she descended to earth she was accompanied by harlots, courtesans and strumpets. Ishtar's lovers were legion and she was the first to indulge in the desires which she inspired. It seems, however, she was not only fickle but cruel as well to those she honored. Even her love affairs with the Gods seemed to end in disaster.

When Ishtar was young, she fell in love with Tammuz, the God of the harvest. It was her love that caused his death. Ishtar was overcome with grief and conceived of a plan to snatch him back from the abode of the dead. It was her descent into the Underworld and subsequent imprisonment that brought death and desolation to the earth. When she was finally released and returned with Tammuz, life once again returned and blossomed forth.

Correspondences (Ishtar)

Archetype:	Virgin, Queen.
Expression:	Divine harlot, patroness of pleasure.
Time:	Full moon.
Season:	Spring.
Objects:	Bow and quiver, sickle of the moon, star.
Number:	Seven.
Colors:	Green, blue-green, sapphire blue.
Animals:	Lion, fish.
Trees:	Apple, cherry.
Plants:	Yarrow, woodruff, violet, orchid, rose, foxglove.
Stones:	Rose quartz, pink tourmaline, emerald, azurite.

Tammuz

Tammuz was a mortal king in whom the God or spirit of fertility was incarnate. He died a violent death. He was an agricultural divinity and vegetation spirit who was manifest in the seed corn.

The myth of Tammuz recounts the cycle of life and death. The God Tammuz is killed by an enemy and his death brings about the stagnation of all natural life. The Goddess, Ishtar, bewailed his death and set out to retrieve him. He was found and liberated with the help of his son. With his resurrection, nature—and especially all vegetation—revived.

Correspondences (Tammuz)

Archetype: Divine victim.
Expression: King, God of the land.
Time: Setting sun.
Season: Fall, winter.
Objects: Cross, scythe, sheaf, flute.
Number: Two
Colors: Gold, orange, brown, green.
Animals: Lion, phoenix, fish.
Trees: Elder, yew, ivy.
Plants: Bay, laurel, corn, frankincense, barley, fumitory, juniper.
Stone: Jasper.

NORSE

Freya

Freya, which means "Lady" is one of the most revered of the Teutonic Goddesses. She was known as the "Fair One" and famed for her great beauty. She is primarily the Goddess of love, but did oversee war, life, and death as well. She is patroness to housewives, mothers, and women of great strength and power. She is one of the demi-Goddesses who selects the most noble of the fallen warriors, which she will then carry to the realm of the Gods.

Freya appeared to her worshipers in a falcon-plumed cloak under which she wore a magical necklace called "Brisingamen." The necklace's power could not be resisted. She would ride through the moonlit sky in a chariot drawn by cats, or sometimes by a huge golden boar.

Freya was wife and priestess to Odin. Although she loved him, and was the protectress of marriages, she was often unfaithful. When Odin left her she wept tears of gold. Then, assuming various names, she searched for him through all the nine Nordic worlds. She slept with dwarves, was delivered into the hands of giants, and then finally she was rescued and returned to the earth.

Correspondences (Freya)

Archetype:	Virgin, lover.
Expression:	Priestess of love, life and death.
Time:	New to full moon.
Seasons:	Spring and summer.
Objects:	Brisingamen, feather cloak, wings.
Number:	Five.
Colors:	Silver, pink, pale blue or green.
Animals:	Cat, hawk, boar.
Trees:	Apple, holly.
Plants:	Cowslip, crocus, rose, lilac, primrose, sweet pea.
Stones:	Blue or pink tourmaline, emerald, chrysocolla.

Odin

Odin was sometimes called Woden or Wotan, which probably meant wild or furious. He was the prime deity of the pantheon and was respected for his vast wisdom. He was considered to be both father and victorious warrior. Because of his authority, he was consulted by all of the other Gods, as well as human beings. Odin was wise in the ways of the world and possessed immense powers.

The myths of Odin describe him as always being involved with the people, taking an interest in their daily lives and helping out in family matters. Often he would roam the world alone, accompanied only by a pair of ravens and a pair of wolves. It is said that he rode upon an eight-legged steed "Slepnir" which represented time itself. He was followed by his son, who personified the yearly rebirth of the spirit of life.

The thing that seems to set Odin apart from other Gods is his quest for knowledge. He treasured it so highly that he gave his right eye for it. At one point he fixed himself to a tree, and hung on it for nine days and nine nights in order to gain wisdom from it. He is the ultimate priest for God, and an example to all humankind because of his ability to gain knowledge.

Correspondences (Odin)

Archetype:	Warrior, father.
Expression:	Priest, Shaman.
Time:	Sunrise.
Season:	Winter.
Objects:	Sword, shield, runes, robe.
Number:	One.
Colors:	Gold, red.
Animals:	Wolf, raven, horse.
Trees:	Birch, oak.
Plants:	Holly, mistletoe, juniper, gum Arabic, marigold, angelica, mastic.
Stones:	Diamond, bloodstone, garnet.

GREEK

Demeter

Demeter was the Goddess of vegetation, fertility, and the fruitful earth. Grain crops were favored by her, especially those of barley and corn. She was the foundress of agriculture and the civic rite of marriage. Her mysteries, which were called the "Thesmophoria," were held each April.

Demeter had several consorts, including Zeus and Poseidon. It was Zeus who tricked her in the form of a bull, making her mother of Persephone. Hades, Demeter's brother, abducted Persephone and took her to the Underworld where he made her his wife. Weeping, Demeter roamed the earth in search of Persephone. During this time the entire world remained barren. Zeus took pity upon the earth and Demeter. He made an agreement with Hades and soon Persephone was returned. This return to the earth brought back spring and all life once again blossomed forth. However, according to the agreement, Persephone had to return and spend one third of the year in the Underworld with her husband, Hades.

Correspondences (Demeter)

Archetype:	Mother, fertility.
Expression:	Patroness of the mysteries.
Time:	Full moon.
Seasons:	Spring, summer.
Objects:	Torch, scepter, water jar, corn dolly.
Numbers:	Three, thirteen.
Colors:	Cornflower blue, yellow, silver.
Animals:	Horse, dolphin, dove.
Tree:	Hawthorne.
Plants:	Corn, barley, bean, sunflower, penny-

	royal, poppy, rose, wheat.
Stone:	Turquoise, peridot, pearl, sapphire, moon stone.

Zeus

Zeus was the supreme deity in Greek mythology. He was the son of Kronos and Rhea, and was considered to be the "wise council." As a composite figure, the sky God of the Greeks was active in the daily concerns of the world. Because of his involvement with humankind's affairs, he was venerated as a ruling father figure, rather than as a creator deity.

Zeus governed the sky and all atmospheric phenomena. He had dominion over the winds, clouds, rain, and the destructive thunder and lightening. He was depicted as a robust and mature man, with wavy or curly hair which matched his thick beard. Zeus often wore a crown of oak leaves, carried a thunderbolt and had an eagle at his feet.

Zeus, like most of the Olympian Gods, had many lovers and begat many children. Some of his unions were with Metis (wisdom), who knew more things than all the Gods and men together. Themis, the daughter of Uranus and Gaia, was another of his loves. She represented the Law that regulates both physical and moral order. He finally married Hera and she became the first lady of Olympus.

Correspondences (Zeus)

Archetype:	Father, ruler/king.
Expression:	Ruler of the sky, king of the Gods.
Time:	Noon to midnight.
Seasons:	Summer, fall and winter.
Objects:	Thunderbolt, scepter, crown, dagger.
Number:	One.

Colors: Royal purple, dark blue, gold.
Animals: Eagle, goat, cuckoo, elephant.
Trees: Oak, poplar, alder.
Plants: Olive, ambergris, violets, apple, mistletoe,
             mastic, fenugreek, mint.
Stones: Diamond, amethyst, chalcedony.

The alcove-altar of Buddha at Our Lady of Enchantment: Buddha found enlightenment while sitting under the Bodhi Tree. He discovered (after starving himself nearly to death for 40 days) that man could not deny the physical to obtain the spiritual. His message is for us to keep balance, seek truth and thereby gain spiritual wisdom.

The correspondences listed for each deity are in actuality symbolic communication links. They serve to attract the specific energies and vibrations to which the deity is aligned. By incorporating their symbols into your rituals, you invite their participation. The following suggestions will help bring you into harmony with your specific God and Goddess:

• Buy a statue of the deity and place it on your altar. Once a day, go before the statue and speak to it as you would a close friend.

• Burn candles in the corresponding colors to the deity statue, or burn them when you are meditating.

• Make a robe of the primary color which corresponds to your deity. Wear this during your meditations and rituals.

• Make a necklace out of the suggested stones to wear during your ceremonies.

• Use the corresponding plants in the incenses and oils you prepare or buy for use during rituals.

• Place the deity's sacred objects on your altar during ritual.

• Incorporate their symbolic animals into your ceremonies or place pictures of them near your ritual area.

• Combine all of the above suggestions and make a shrine to your deity so the energy is available when you wish to work with it.

CHAPTER SIX

Circles and Cycles

A Practical Approach to Ritual

There have been vast amounts of research done on the moon, establishing its affect on both humans and the environment. It has been credited with the curious power of being able to change humans into beasts, vampires into bats, and the most cautious people into passionate lovers. As it seems to be held in such awesome regard, the lunar cycle will be the first to consider.

The moon, like the sun, appears to rise in the east and set in the west. Unlike the sun, the appearance of its size and shape continually change, at least from our earthbound perspective. There are four cycles of approximately seven days each in a lunar month. The phases the moon goes through include the *Dark of the Moon* (also called the *New Moon*). It waxes and grows larger until the *first quarter* is visible as the Half Moon. When the moon waxes or grows larger, its horns point to the east until it reaches a full circle known as the *Full Moon*. It will then begin to diminish in size as it wanes through the *last quarter*, with the horns pointing west.

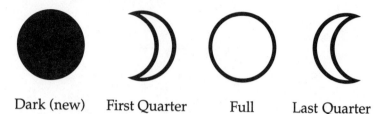

Dark (new)   First Quarter   Full   Last Quarter

Knowing the phases of the moon will help you plan your rituals. Rituals always work best when they are in agreement with corresponding planetary energies. It is important to time magical operations according to the phases of the moon so that you stay in *sympathy* with the natural pull of the universe. By doing this you combine natural outside energy and power with your own energy and power. When doing magic, the more circumstances you can bring into harmony with what you are doing, the better the results will be.

By looking at the phases of the moon one at time we can see an inherent working pattern evolve. The period from New through the first quarter is usually referred to as the Waxing Moon. This is the best time to begin new projects and to work towards obtaining something on a positive level. Symbolically this is the Goddess' virgin aspect. It relates to the East, air, intellect, and intuition.

During the Full Moon, projects already begun are energized, nurtured and reaffirmed. This phase of the moon relates to the West and the mother Goddess aspect.

During the last quarter to Dark Moon is a time of contemplation, reflection and negation. It is a time associated with the crone aspect and is a good time to consider our actions, release negative energies, rest, and regenerate the mind and body. This phase of the moon is aligned to the West and the North. Dark Moon is a very good time to get rid of things which are negative. A time to let go of petty judgments and hatreds, cleanse and purify our surroundings.

There are many ways to work with these combinations. I like to begin with the Dark Moon, which is the time just before New Moon. This is a good time to get rid of negative energies which may surround me or my goal. Then, when New Moon arrives I am able to begin working on something positive, without the influence of unwanted vibrations. I will then use the Full Moon to emphasize and reaffirm that which I have already set in motion. Finally, the last quarter is used for contemplation and gives the goal time to manifest.

A good example of this is people who wish to bring love into their life. At Dark Moon they would work on getting rid of their personal fears about love. Or, if they were doing a ritual to attract someone they already knew, they would use this time for dissipating their fears about love and relationships. When the moon begins to wax they would work on becoming more attractive to the other person, or building self-esteem. On the night of the Full Moon, they would put all of their energy into proclaiming their desire and concentrating on how the loved one should see or react to them.

Each Full Moon has a specific designation and symbolic meaning. As can be seen by the following list, these meanings are obviously connected to the hunting and agricultural seasons of our ancestors. However, just because their meanings may be slightly antiquated does not necessarily make them obsolete. Energy is energy, and though we may not be using it for procreation of the tribe or a bumper crop of corn, we can surely use it for the advancement of intellectual and spiritual endeavors.

The Full Moons

November—SNOW MOON: Scorpio brings in the dark season and winter begins. This is the death of the season and time to get rid of negative thoughts and vibrations.

December—OAK MOON: The mighty oak withstands the cold hardship of winter. The oak is revered because of its longevity and the fact that such a mighty creature comes from the smallest acorn. Now is the time to remain steadfast in convictions and principles.

January—WOLF MOON: The wolf is a fearsome creature of the night as well as being a companion to the God of the hunt. As the God-force, or Lord of light, has just been reborn, the wolf protects. This is a time to protect what we have, as well as consider new options.

February—STORM MOON: A storm is said to rage most fiercely just before it ends, and the year usually follows suit. Winter, death and darkness are coming to an end. It is now time to plan for the future and what we will pursue in the months to come.

March—CHASTE MOON: The Goddess returns in her virgin aspect and we should greet her with a clear mind and heart. This marks the end of winter and uncertainty. Now we can begin to plant the seeds of desire.

April—SEED MOON: Spring is in the air, all is green and speaks of growth. This is the time of sowing seeds (spiritual or physical) and the time to physically put our desires into motion.

May—HARE MOON: The hare was sacred to the Goddess, springtime, and fertility. Now, with all life blossoming about us, the creative spirit takes over as we reaffirm our goals.

June—DYAD MOON: Dyad is the Latin name for pair, the twin stars of Castor Pollux. This is a time of equality, union of opposites, and duality. It is the time to seek balance between our spiritual and physical desires.

July—MEAD MOON: Mead was the traditional beverage of our European ancestors. This was a time used for working to preserve some of those crops (mostly for wine and ale-making) for winter and future use. It is the time to plan for what we will do when we reach our goals.

August—WORT MOON: Wort is the Anglo-Saxon term for herb or green plant. This is the first harvest and a time to celebrate as well as work toward reaching our goal. Plans for preserving what we have attained should be considered.

September—BARLEY MOON: We enter the sign of Virgo, the virgin who carries sheaves of barely and grain. This is the Great Harvest, a time for celebration and realization of desired goals.

October—BLOOD MOON: This moon marked the season of hunting and the slaughter of the animals for winter food and clothing. Blood is the force of life. Now is the time to offer up the reddest of wine in thanksgiving to the deities for what we have attained.

The phases of the moon are not the only things to keep in mind when planning the best time to do something. The seven days of the week and their corresponding planetary affiliations are also useful. The list presented here outlines the natural-magical correspondences of these astrological energies. Whereas the moon gives us an indication of when the work should ideally be done, the planets give us the day—as well as some symbolic, vibrational considerations, which add strength and power to our rituals.

Sunday—SUN: This is a day of high masculine solar energy. A very powerful time and one good for individual, positive, creative works. Begin things related to acquiring money, health, friendship and patronage for business. The element for Sunday is fire; the color is yellow/gold or gold. The numerical consideration is six. Marigolds, sunflowers, and goldenrod are associated with this planetary influence, as well as the precious metal gold, the diamond, topaz, and tiger's eye.

Monday—MOON: This is a day of goddess-oriented, all-feminine energy. High energy is directed towards all matters concerning conception, development of emotional self-expression, seeking inspiration, enhancing psychic abilities, initiating changes, and enhancing personal growth of the feminine aspect. The element for Monday is water; the color is silver or white. The numerical consideration is nine. Watercress, jasmine, and moon flower are associated with this planet, along with the metal silver, the moonstone, pearl and clear quartz crystal.

Tuesday—MARS: Dynamic energy is the only way to express Mars. It is pure raw power and intense activity. This is a good time to overcome rivalry or enmity, develop physical strength and courage, or protect one's property and investments. It is good for military matters and anything which requires a lot of force, power, and energy to activate. It is very masculine in gender and warlike in presentation. The element for Tuesday is fire; the color is red, vivid blood-red. The numerical consideration is five. Wormwood, pepper, and garlic are associated with this planet, along with iron, bloodstone, ruby and garnet.

Wednesday—MERCURY: Communication is the key for Mercury. This planet wants to be heard and will aid you in getting your ideas out there; it's good for business deals and helping to influence others—very career oriented. The element for Wednesday is air; the color is yellow. The numerical consideration is eight. Cinnamon, horehound, and honesty are associated with this planet, along with quicksilver (mercury), opal, agate and aventurine.

Thursday—JUPITER: Jupiter deals with expansion, idealism, and ambition. Jupiter will help you attain friendship. It is good to use for career success and all situations concerned with money. Legal transactions are best dealt with during Jupiter. Religious expansion is also expressed through this planet. The element for Thursday is water and the color is deep blue or purple. The numerical consideration is four. Cedar, betony, and mistletoe are associated with this planet along with tin, amethyst, lepidolite and lapis lazuli.

Friday—VENUS: Love and attraction are the key words for Venus. All works involving sensual and sexual attraction are in her domain. It is a good time to create a union between opposites and build good relationships. The element for Friday can be either earth or water and the color is green. The numerical consideration is seven. Rose, basil and yarrow are associated with this planet along with copper, rose quartz, emerald and chrysocolla.

Saturday—SATURN: Formation and the first law of karma (limitation) belong to Saturn. Here we find the tester, and the principle of learning through trial and error; Saturn should be used to preserve, stabilize and crystalize our ability to discipline ourselves. The element for Saturday is earth and the color is black. The numerical consideration is three. Hemlock, skullcap, spikenard and belladonna are all associated with this planet, along with onyx, black tourmaline, obsidian and jet.

Of primary importance to the execution of a proper ritual is having a suitable place to perform the magical event. This need not be an elaborate, ostentatious setting which is costly and burdensome to maintain. Everyone has a place to do ritual and should take the time to respectfully prepare said space. The physical setting is as important as proper ritual construction. You do not see a doctor attempting to do an operation in a dirty, disorganized setting. Ritual is no different. Everything needs to be clean, neat and aesthetically pleasing to get good results. For the most part, magic rituals are usually executed within the bounds of a circle. There may be reasons for this.

The circle is a universal symbol of totality, wholeness, and original perfection. It has no beginning and it has no end. It is in itself the unmanifest, the infinite eternal, and a time-enclosed space. It represents celestial unity, cyclic movement, and completion. The circle is feminine in nature and serves to contain, as does the womb, all life and energy raised within. It also provides a limit or boundary in the creation of sacred space.

Bearing the symbology of the circle in mind, the first objective is to find a suitable location, some place where a circle could be created in physical form. This can be done in several different ways. You can create a circle by taking a large length of cord or heavy string and marking off the actual area, by sewing or painting the form of a circle onto a rug or piece of cloth, or by just inscribing the circle directly onto the floor with tape or paint. I have even seen some people use small stones or rocks to create the circle.

The size of the circle will, of course, depend upon the area available. Even though some say it must be nine feet in diameter and others insist on thirteen feet, size really doesn't matter. What counts is continuity and visibility of an actual physical circle. It needs to be a space set aside, in which you can comfortably move around and it must be dedicated to sacred work.

Next in line of importance is the altar, for this will be the surface on which you will be working. The altar is usually placed in the center of the circle and therefore becomes the point of focus for your ceremonies. However, at times the altar can be set in one of the four directions. For example, should you be working on developing personal power, you might want to put the altar in the South, for fire energy; or perhaps the East, for new beginnings or spiritual atonement. Consider the purpose of the ritual when deciding the orientation of the altar.

To the magician or spiritual practitioner, the altar is of extreme importance. It provides the foundation or form on which to build and execute magical works. The altar is where all obeisance is directed and focused during ritual. This is why you see such imposing altars in churches and cathedrals. The priests of old understood the laws of the universe and knew how to best utilize the energy of those who came to pray and worship. They literally captivated their audience with the beauty and majesty of lavish, flamboyant props. Once they had the members' complete attention, they were able to direct the power raised through the Mass toward their desired goal. It is not hard to see how the Catholic church was able to become such a prominent organization. It had thousands of people, for hundreds of years, giving it their energy.

The personal altar is of no less importance than the most elegant one found in a cathedral. All altars should reflect the individual's personality, be clean and neat, as well as aesthetically pleasing. It is the altar which provides the backdrop for the ritual, establishes the theme, and helps set the mood of the ceremony. In most cases it is the focal point of the ritual, the place where all energy is directed.

The altar, in an esoteric sense, becomes an extension of your mind and creative process. This is where the substance of thought takes on physical form. The altar allows you to express (through props used on the material plane) that which you wish to bring about. In other words, it allows you to stand aside and look directly at your intentions. It represents your thoughts in an objective-physical arrangement. Each item, including the altar itself, symbolizes a segment of your extended ability, power, and ambition. The altar is desire made manifest.

Altars, like people, come in all shapes and sizes. No two are really alike. For the outdoor enthusiast, a large flat stone or tree stump may serve as the altar. The picnic basket with a flat top also works well and has the ability to transport all of the necessary items needed as well. If you are cramped for space, a nicely carved chest or end table with drawers can be the answer, as the top will serve for the working surface and all the tools can be kept inside when not in use. Even folding trays and tables can be used for altars. Be creative, use your imagination, just be conscious of the fact the altar reflects back to your higher consciousness your creative ability.

Another important point to remember when setting up your altar is only put on it what you need to do the work at hand. There is nothing more distracting than a table filled with this and that and some of everything. More is not necessarily better. When it comes to magic, more often creates confusion. The whole point of doing ritual with tools and an altar is to distract the ego and capture the attention of the higher consciousness through a single effort. We don't want to bewilder it to the point of stupefication with physical objects.

Some Symbolic Suggestions

Each category of ritual will have certain unique symbols which make the ceremony special. This helps the consciousness to direct and focus its energy toward the desired and represented goal. To help you select things to use in ritual that will be most appropriate to the goal, I have provided the following list of suggestions.

Love and Happiness

For a love ritual, the following items speak directly to the heart and help create a loving vibration:

Rose quartz, pink candles, any type of a heart-shaped box; rose or pink altar cloth, a cup or chalice filled with honey wine or a sweet beverage; rose, cherry or apple blossom incense; a lace fan, pink and white flowers, heart-shaped jewelry; pink feathers, and any type of sweet fragrant oil.

Money and Prosperity

To help with money problems, such as getting a raise in pay, you might wish to use: Gold coins, yellow or gold candles, a round box painted gold or yellow; yellow or gold altar cloth, a yellow pouch to carry attraction stones (such as topaz, citrine, cat's eye or amber); a dollar bill placed on the pentacle with a gold candle on top of it, gold glitter; amber, orange blossom, or honeysuckle incense; gold jewelry, marigolds, and a richly-scented perfume or oil.

Strength and Personal Power

To help regain personal power or express aggressive action, force, and control, the following items could be helpful:

Red candles and altar cloth, the sword or athame; bloodstone, diamond, garnet; symbols or objects relating to the planet Mars; red carnations, cinnamon or dragon's blood incense; fire contained in a small pot, red clothing, candlesticks shaped like towers, snakes or weapons.

Prophecy and Psychic Power

For setting up a divination altar to enhance your psychic powers you might wish to use:

Blue candles; blue and white flowers such as gardenias and violets; amethyst, lapis lazuli and fluorite; the wand and incense burner; lavender, lily or myrrh incense; galangal oil; crystal ball; Tarot cards or other divination objects; bells, light string or wind instrument music.

These are just some suggestions as to what can be placed on an altar or used to help set the mood for a specific ritual. Use your imagination and those items and objects which have meaning to you.

CHAPTER SEVEN

First Steps in Ritual

Preparation of Tools and Sacred Space

Magic is to be experienced, not just intellectualized. It is a system in which the practitioner learns by doing. One of the first things you will want to learn to do is how to purify and consecrate your working tools. Purification removes all previous forces and vibrations from the tools. Consecration infuses them with your own personal thoughts and feelings.

Purification and consecration are an integral part of ritual magic. They clear away the negativity and they help set the vibratory frequency for the projection of personal power. These special ceremonies help you personalize ritual objects and attune them to your own physical and psychic energies. It is this psychic rapport with the tools which turns them into extensions of your personal magnetism.

The best time to do a ritual of purification and consecration is during the Waxing Moon. This is the time of new beginnings, when the creative energies are most active. The Waxing Moon also provides a positive force field with which to work. As the consecration of the tools is a positive activity and the beginning of your magical work, it is best done during this lunar phase.

The rituals of purification and consecration are simple and don't require much previous experience. All you really need are the items listed below, a quiet space, and some time alone. Read through both rituals several times, make note of what is taking place, and create your ritual check list.

Before you begin, review each of the rituals. Using your check list, double-check to make sure you have everything you need. Once everything is set you will want to take a *pre-ritual bath*. This will wash away any negativity you have picked up during the day, as well as help relax and prepare you for ritual. All you need for the ritual bath is some salt, a white candle and a stick of sandalwood incense.

The Ritual Bath

As the bath water is running, light the white candle saying:

> *Let the Spirit of Fire*
> *Now consume all harmful energies*
> *Within and without.*

Light the incense as you say:

> *May this essence of Air*
> *Purify my mind and soul.*

Sprinkle the salt into the bath water saying:

Now let the elements of Earth and Water
Combine to cleanse and protect me from
All negative thoughts and vibrations.

Relax, and enjoy this quiet time alone. Allow yourself
to let go of all the contrary thoughts or happenings of the
day. Meditate on what you will be doing in the ritual.
When you let the water out of the tub, visualize all of the
uncleanliness and negative vibrations which may have
been attached to you going down the drain. You are now
clean and ready to proceed with the ceremony.

The salt and water bowls. These are made of silver. These bowls
and the athame are used for consecrating the elements and casting the
circle.

The Ritual of Purification

For this simple ritual you will need the following items: a small table or altar covered with a white cloth, one white candle, a small bowl of salt, a small bowel of water, some sandalwood incense, and a small dish filled with sand (or a censor) in which to burn the incense.

Gather up all of your tools and place them on the altar.

Incense (air), to represent your intellectual attributes, should be placed on the *Eastern* corner of the table.

Candle (fire), to represent your strength and personal power, should be placed on the *Southern* corner of the table.

Water (water) to represent your emotions and intuition, is placed on the *Western* corner of the table.

Salt (earth) to represent the ability to manifest your desires, is placed on the *Northern* corner of the table.

Once this has been done you are ready to begin. Be sure that you have all of your tools with you. These can be placed on top of or under the table, depending on available space.

Begin by relaxing. Focus your attention and visualize the immediate area enclosed in a large cone of light; feel the cone surrounding you completely, forming a protective barrier between you and the outside world. When you become comfortable with the cone of protection, visualize a shaft of blue-white light (the true spirit of the cosmos) flowing in through the top of the cone; spiraling downward and bathing you in its pure vital energy. This active visualization will force all of the negative energies away from you and out the bottom of the floor of the cone. When you feel completely safe, protected and energized, it is time to begin the actual purification of the tools.

Take several deep, relaxing breaths. Pick up the wand and pass it through the incense smoke and candle flame, then sprinkle it with water and salt. *Focus your attention*, see all the negative thoughts and vibrations being drawn out of the tool and dispersed. (Repeat with each tool.) As you do this say the following:

> *Magic Staff, Air Wand, Instrument of Intelligence, Insight and Wisdom, let now*
> *The powers of Air, Fire, Water and Earth cleanse thee of all negative thoughts and vibrations.*

Now place the wand next to the incense and pick up the dagger or sword. Focus your attention on the knife as you pass it through each of the elements. Visualize all negativity flowing out of it as you say:

> *Magic Sword, Fire Dagger, Blade of Strength, Sovereignty and Protection, let now the powers of Air, Fire, Water and Earth cleanse thee of all negative thoughts and vibrations.*

Place the dagger next to the candle. Pick up the chalice. Focus your attention on the chalice as you pass it through each of the elements, visualize all negative thoughts leaving as you recite:

> *Magic Cup, Grail of Immortality, Vessel of Love, Emotional Strength and Regeneration, let now the powers of Air, Fire, Water and Earth cleanse thee of all negative thoughts and vibrations.*

Place the chalice next to the water. Pick up the pentacle. Focus your attention on the pentacle as you pass it through each of the elements. Visualize all negative thoughts leaving as you recite:

> *Magic Disk, Earth Matrix, Shield of Fortitude, Emblem of my Creative Foundation, let now the*

powers of Air, Fire, Water and Earth cleanse thee
of all negative thoughts and vibrations.

Place the pentacle next to the salt.

The incense burner is used to represent the element of Air. This one is made of brass and is fairly ornate. It came from an import store.

Once you have cleansed each of the tools, take a moment to reflect. Look at the them in conjunction with the elements with which they are aligned. Feel the energy of the element in the tool.

Pick up your wand. See and feel it in the association with air, how the shaft of it will soon contain your thoughts and inspirations. Know the sword has absorbed the element of fire, giving it strength and the ability to protect. Appreciate the beauty of the chalice, allow it to bring forth hidden emotions that will aid you in your work. Notice how stable the disk is, it even resembles a foundation, one that you soon will begin to build upon.

The Ritual of Consecration

Once the tools are clean, they are ready to be consecrated, or blessed and dedicated, to your purpose. They will serve as extensions of your magical will to help you focus and direct energy. Because of this, they should be filled with your own personal thoughts and vibrations in accordance with the natural elements they each represent.

Beginning with the wand, hold each tool in your strongest hand (right if right-handed and left if left-handed). Feel the alignment the tool has with the element it represents. Allow this feeling to flow through you and back into the tool. For example: feel the light airiness of the wand, feel how it inspires you to do really great things. You know that when you have it in your hand all things are possible. It truly is magical.

Pick up the wand and hold it at eye level. Visualize the power and force of the cosmos, in the form of a blue flame, coming into it. At the same time, feel your own personal energy and power coming up from within you and going into the wand. You are now combining your energy with that of the universe and instilling it into the wand. Do this with each tool in turn as you say and feel the appropriate words:

WAND

I now bless and consecrate thee
Magical Tool, Wand of Enlightenment,
That thou shall ever serve me in
Truth, Power and Wisdom.
So mote it be!

SWORD *(Athame)*

I now bless and consecrate thee
Magical Tool, Lance of Sovereignty,
That thou shall ever serve me in
Truth, Power and Wisdom.
So mote it be!

CHALICE

I now bless and consecrate thee
Magical Tool, Grail of Immortality
That thou shall ever serve me in
Truth, Power and Wisdom.
So mote it be!

PENTACLE

I now bless and consecrate thee
Magical Tool, Shield of Honor
That thou shall ever serve me in
Truth, Power and Wisdom.
So mote it be!

This concludes the purification and consecration ritual. Take a moment to reflect, then allow yourself to relax and let go of the cone of protection you have created. Inhale and exhale to the count of five. Each time you do this, see and feel more of the surrounding cone dissipating, going into the ground, leaving you feeling refreshed and energized.

Creating Sacred Space

Creating sacred space is an essential part of all magical operations. The actual act itself takes the form of casting or constructing a magic circle. This is done in order to create the proper environment for magical rites. Once the magic circle has been created, it will protect the individuals within its boundary from outside negative influence. The circle, or boundary, will also help contain the energy raised within its periphery until the time of release.

The first thing you will want to do is to clearly mark out a circle on the floor. The ideal size of a magical circle is nine feet, but this is ideal, not mandatory. Nine is preferred because it is made from the all-powerful 3 x 3. It is the triple triad and represents completion, fulfillment, attainment, beginning and end, the whole. In most cases, the size of the circle will depend on available space and the amount of people taking part in the ritual. Obviously five to seven people will fit nicely into a nine-foot circle, fifty will not.

The actual marking of the circle can be done in a variety of ways. If the floor is carpeted, you can mark the circle with tape or string. Hardwood, cement, or tile can be marked with light colored chalk. If you are working outside then you can mark the earth with your wand or athame. For those who have a special room set aside for their magical practice, the circle may be painted directly onto the floor itself. A large piece of indoor-outdoor carpet cut into a circle serves nicely and can be rolled up and stored when you are finished. Seasonal representations, such as flowers, pine cones or small sprigs of greenery are a welcome touch. The important thing is not so much what you use but the actual physical setting of a boundary line.

Symbolizing the Four Quadrants

Once the circle is marked, you will want to acknowledge the four quadrants or elemental directions with a symbolic representation. The four quadrants represent the four elements of nature and their respective energies. The East is air, intellect, and new beginnings; the South is fire, power, and the force within; the West is water, emotion, and rebirth; the North is earth and our ability to manifest desire. The following list will give you some ideas, some possibilities of things to use to represent the four quadrants.

East: Incense burner and a joss stick or cone incense, blue candle, large piece of amethyst, the Star card of the Tarot, blue circle.

South: Candle holder with a red candle, garnet or bloodstone, the Strength card of the Tarot, red triangle.

West: Goblet filled with water, green candle, aquamarine or green tourmaline, the Death card of the Tarot, green crescent moon.

North: A square wooden box with a Pentacle engraved on the top, clear quartz crystal, yellow candle, the Hierophant card of the Tarot, yellow square.

Place those objects symbolizing the quadrants on the floor outside of the circle, in the appropriate direction. Use small tables or boxes to hold the items, or place them on wall shelves which correspond to the proper direction.

The East quadrant in the Chapel at Our Lady of Enchantment: Banner with astrological and Air symbols, statue of Kuan-Yin the Madonna of East Asia, incense burner and blue candle (all Air symbols).

The South quadrant in the Chapel at Our Lady of Enchantment: Banner with astrological and Fire symbols, statue of Christ as the sun god and divine victim, red candle and sword below to symbolize the strength, power and divine spark within us all.

The North quadrant in the Chapel at Our Lady of Enchantment: Banner with astrological and Earth symbols, statue of Buddha (who is associated with balance), a yellow candle, and the pentacle—all representing our ability to create through balance.

The West quadrant in the Chapel of Our Lady of Enchantment: Banner with astrological and Water symbols, statue of Selket who is associated with the Egyptian Underworld. There is a chalice with water and a green candle, representing water and transformation.

The main altar, dedicated to the Goddess, in the Chapel at Our Lady of Enchantment: To the right are the Stang (symbol of the God) and the Cauldron (representing the Goddess).

When the circle and directions are clearly marked on the floor, place the altar inside of the circle. The position of the altar in the circle is up to the individual. However, most practitioners tend to favor keeping it in the center, facing either *North* or *East*. North represents the realm of the Gods and manifestation; the East is new beginnings and the realm of the spirit. By placing it in the center of the circle it automatically becomes the focal point of the ceremony where all energy and power is directed. As the altar represents the core of our desire, its central location will only enhance the work at hand.

The next step is the actual casting of the magic circle. This is accomplished in two parts: first, the consecration of the elements (salt and water) and second, the projecting of energy onto the marked circle. These combined actions produce the proper atmosphere for a ritual. It is important to understand that as you project the energy onto the physical circle line, you are in reality creating a sphere or total enclosure, rather than just a flat line of energy. When properly completed you will feel as though you are inside a large ball of protective light.

Instructions for Casting the Circle

STEP 1. Take your athame or wand, dip the tip into the water saying:

> *Creature of Water, cast out from thyself all impurities and uncleanliness of this world.*

STEP 2. Dip your athame or wand into the salt saying:

> *Creature of Earth, let only good enter to aid me in my work.*

STEP 3. Stir three scoops of salt into the water, see with your mind's eye all the negativity leaving. Now, holding your athame or wand in front of you, begin to visualize the energy in the form of a blue flame, coming through into the point of the wand or athame. Begin walking in a deosil (clockwise) manner, pointing your athame or wand down at the edge of the circle as you say:

> *I conjure and create thee, O Circle of Power. Be thou a boundary between the world of Men and the realm of the Mighty Ones, a Sphere of Protection to preserve and contain all powers raised within. Let now this Circle be a place of Peace, Love and Power. So mote it be.*

With the casting of the circle completed, you will then want to acknowledge the four directions or quadrants. This can be done in several ways. Whether the method be simple or complex, the idea is to enlist these specific energies to guard and protect your circle. There are two methods that we will describe. The first is a simple acknowledgment of the quadrants and is done prior to the casting of the circle. This method can be used for personal works, or ones where the circle itself serves as the majority of protection.

Acknowledgment of the Quadrants

For this particular method you will need to have candles at each of the quadrants: for the East, blue; the South, red; West, green; North, yellow.

Stand before the altar, take several deep, relaxing breaths. When you feel composed and ready, proceed to the Eastern quadrant with a lighted taper. Pick up the Eastern candle, light it as you say the following:

> *I light the East, the home of Moonlight and Consciousness, the realm of the Spirit.*

Now proceed to the South; light the candle as you say the following:

> *I light the South, the home of Fire and Inspiration, the realm of Awareness.*

Now proceed to the West; light the candle as you say the following:

> *I light the West, the home of the Waves, of Completeness, the realm of our Watery Beginnings.*

Now proceed to the North; light the candle as you say the following:

> *I light the North, the home of All that is Green and Fruitful, the realm of Remembrance.*

Now return to the altar, consecrate the elements, and cast the circle.

Calling In of the Guardians

The following procedure is for the actual calling in of protective Guardians. Guardians are highly evolved soul-minds who are attached or attracted to the earth vibration. They can be Archangels (etheric world intelligences who have always existed) or Higher Energy Forces in alignment with archetypal elemental forms. This ritual to call in the Guardians is usually done for Full Moon rituals and Sabbats, or any time a great amount of protection and extra energy is needed.

For this you will need four candles, one for each quadrant in its corresponding color, and something symbolic to represent the quadrant as well. On the altar you will need a white votive to represent the Spirit. Once the circle has been cast, return to the altar. Take several deep breaths, relax, and then proceed to the Eastern quadrant (again walking deosil) with your athame. Point the athame upwards in the direction of the quadrant and visualize the Guardian approaching.

Light the blue candle of the East and say:

> *Hear me, O Mighty One, Ruler of the Whirlwinds,*
> *Guardian of the Eastern Portal. Let your essence be*
> *as one with me (ours), as Witness and Shield at this*
> *Gateway between the Worlds. So mote it be.*

Hold the Eastern symbol in offering, replace it, and then proceed to the South.

Light the red candle of the South and say:

> *Hear me, O Mighty One, Ruler of the Solar Orb,*
> *Guardian of the Southern Portal. Let your light be*
> *as one with me (ours), as Witness and Shield at this*
> *Gateway between the Worlds. So mote it be.*

Hold the Southern symbol in offering, replace it and then proceed to the West.

Light the green candle of the West and say:

> *Hear me, O Mighty One, Ruler of the Mysterious*
> *Depths, Guardian of the Western Portal. Let your*
> *fluid be as one with me (ours) as Witness and*
> *Shield at this Gateway between the Worlds. So*
> *mote it be.*

Hold the Western symbol in offering, replace it and proceed to the North.

Light the yellow candle of the North and say:

> *Hear me, O Mighty One, Ruler of the Forest and Field, Guardian of the Northern Portal. Let your fruitfulness be as one with me (ours) as Witness and Shield at this Gateway between the Worlds. So mote it be.*

Now hold the Northern symbol in offering, replace it and return to the altar, and light the white votive. Address the fifth element of the Spirit as follows:

> *Hear me O Mighty One, Ruler of the Heavenly Vault, Guardian of the Divine Kingdom. Let your wisdom be as one with ours. For as above, so below, so the Universe, so the Soul. As without, as within, let our rite now begin. So mote it be.*

At this point, your temple is erected and sacred space has been created. Once inside your circle you will not want to step outside until your ritual is completed, the Guardians dismissed, and the circle banished.

Dismissing the Guardians

The following method is for dismissing the Guardians and taking up the circle. This is done to release and clear the area of the raised vibrations and energy.

You will begin in the North and proceed widdershins (counter-clockwise) around the circle.

> *Hear me, O Mighty One, Ruler of Forest and Field, Guardian of the Northern Portal. I (we) thank thee for thy Blessings and Protection and bid thee hail and farewell.*

Now put the Northern candle out and proceed to the West.

> *Hear me, O Mighty One, Ruler of the Mysterious Depths, Guardian of the Western Portal. I (we) thank thee for thy Blessings and Protection and bid thee hail and farewell.*

Now put the Western candle out and proceed to the South.

> *Hear me O Mighty One, Ruler of the Solar Orb, Guardian of the Southern Portal. I (we) thank thee for thy Blessings and Protection and bid thee hail and farewell.*

Now put out the Southern candle and proceed to the East.

> *Hear me, O Mighty One, Ruler of the Whirlwinds, Guardian of the Eastern Portal. I (we) thank thee for thy Blessings and Protection and bid thee hail and farewell.*

Now put out the Eastern candle and proceed back to the altar to address Spirit.

> *Hear me, O Mighty One, Ruler of the Heavenly Vault, Guardian of the Divine Kingdom. I (we) thank thee for thy Blessings and Protection and bid thee hail and farewell.*

Banishing the Circle

Now put out the white votive representing the Spirit. You will now want to banish the circle. Begin in the North and proceed in a widdershins (counter-clockwise) manner around the circle, this time drawing the energy back up into the wand or athame:

> *O Circle of Power that has been a boundary be-tween the World of Men and the Realm of the Mighty One, that has served to Preserve and Pro-tect, I now release all powers raised within and banish Thee , O Circle of Power. So mote it be.*

With the banishing of the circle, the rite is brought to a close. If you do not have a special room set aside for rit-ual, it is a good idea to get into the habit of putting your magical tools away immediately. Another suggestion is post-ritual celebration. Many practitioners like to have a feast following special ceremonies. This helps to ground everyone as well as provide a social time for relaxed dis-cussion about the ritual and related subjects.

A Full Moon Ritual

This basic Full Moon ritual is designed for a group. For the individual practitioner it may be slightly lengthy and involved. Those working alone will find a complete solitary Full Moon ritual in Appendix II. All speaking parts are marked as follows: (LF) Female Leader, (LM) Male Leader, (C) for Celebrant. The part of Celebrant can be given to more than one individual so more members may participate.

The Ritual of the Full Moon

Time: Night of the Full Moon
Items Needed: White altar candles, chalice, athame, a bowl of salt and one of water, cakes and wine for blessing, in-cense burner and incense, pentacle, working candle, quadrant candles, matches, charcoal, and a bell.

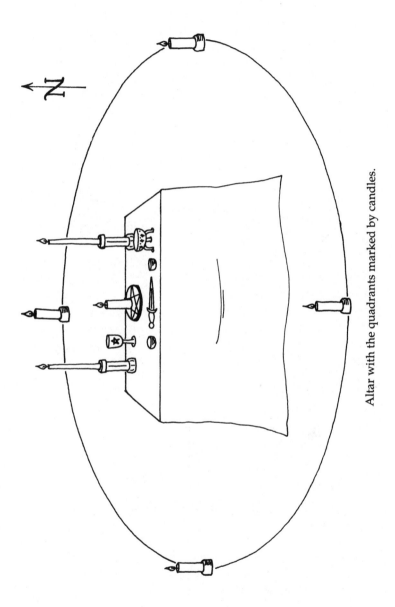

Altar with the quadrants marked by candles.

(C) The Celebrant comes forward to the altar, genuflects or bows in respect, and then lights the altar candles, saying the following:

> (While lighting the right candle): *Holy art thou, Lord of the Universe, for you are our Power and Might.*

> (While lighting the left candle): *Holy art thou Lady of All Creation, for you are our Life and Light.*

(LF) The Lead Female will now consecrate the elements (as per instructions given previously) and cast the circle.

(LM) The Lead Male will now call in the Guardians by lighting their respective candles and addressing them as per instructions.

(LF) The Lead Female will now invoke the Goddess (invocation to Cerridwen is in Appendix I).

(LM) The Lead Male Faces the altar and speaks the following:

> *Lord and Lady of the night,*
> *Of mist and of moonlight.*
> *Eternal Mother of the Silver Wheel,*
> *Father at whose altar we kneel.*
> *Guide each of us in work and deed,*
> *And grant to us that which we need.*

(LF) The Lead Female faces the altar and speaks the following:

> *Hear us Cerridwen and Cernunnos*
> *The time of magic draws near,*
> *Hear us Lord and Lady, hear the*
> *Invoking words we pray, and appear.*

For with arms outstretched,
We stand in your light
And beseech thee,
Grant that our magic works this night.

(All Members)

Ayea, ayea, Cerridwen
Ayea, ayea, Cerridwen
Ayea, ayea, Cerridwen
Ayea, ayea, ayea!

Ayea, ayea, Cernunnos
Ayea, ayea, Cernunnos
Ayea, ayea, Cernunnos
Ayea, ayea, ayea!

(Ayea is pronounced "I-A." It is an archaic term meaning "hail to" or "in honor." Cerridwen is the Celtic Moon and Grain Goddess, owner of the inexhaustible cauldron of magic and regeneration. Cernunnos is the Celtic Horned God of animals, nature, and fecundity.)

(C) The Celebrant tones the bell three times and picks up the working candle. She or he then lights the candle and speaks the following while holding it in offering to the Gods:

Hail to thee Great Mother,
Divine triple muse,
In thee are all things reconciled,
In thee are all things held in harmony,
In thee are love and truth united.
Be thou clothed in light,
Thou who shall be our guide through the ages.
So shall it be!

(C) Now the Celebrant takes the working candle to each of the quadrants. The Celebrant walks deosil (clockwise) and beginning in the East will offer the candle up and speak at each quadrant:

(East) *Let our thoughts be clear.*

(South) *Let our actions be strong.*

(West) *Let our emotions be controlled.*

(North) *Let our desires come into manifestation.*

(C) Now the Celebrant places the candle on the altar and all members take hands and raise energy for their desired work by chanting the following:

Lovely Lady of the Moon,
Grant our needs and wishes soon.

(C) The celebrant tones the bell three times and the Lead Female (LF) and Lead Male (LM) do the Blessings of the Cakes and Wine (see Appendix I for Blessing Cakes and Wine) for all to partake in *perfect love and perfect trust.*
(LM) The Lead Male now genuflects or bows before the altar and will speak the closing prayer:

Blessed be our Lady,
Mother of all,
Thou who was before mankind,
Thou art our inspiration and hope,
For thou hast been with us from the beginning
And shall be with us at the end of time,
I ask your blessings this day.
Be with us now and forever.
So shall it be!

(LM) The Lead Male will now dismiss the Guardians, beginning in the North and proceeding widdershins (counter-clockwise) to the West as per instructions.

(LF) The Lead Female will now banish the circle in a widdershins manner as per instructions.

(C) The Celebrant will now extinguish the altar candles while saying the following:

> *(Left) Our lady of life and light,*
> *We bid thee hail and farewell this night.*

> *(Right) Our lord of power and might*
> *We bid thee hail and farewell this night.*

The rite is now ended. The working candle should be left to burn out completely and all other items should be put away.

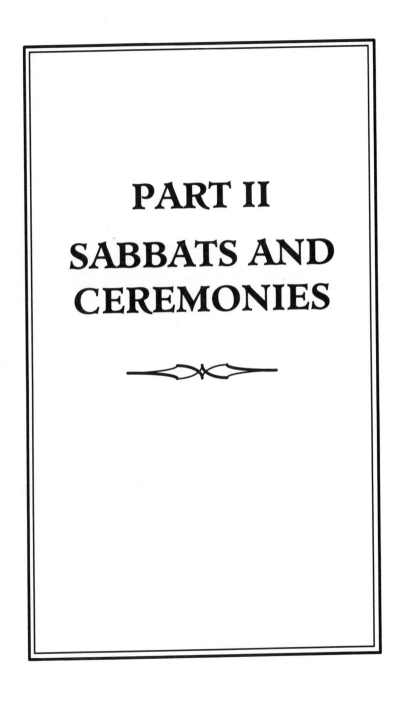

PART II
SABBATS AND CEREMONIES

CHAPTER EIGHT

Reclaiming the Power

The Path of
Least Resistance

Just like water, electricity, or any other form of energy, magic travels the path of least resistance. This is why you look for the way which offers the least amount of opposition to your magical operation. By working with the path of least resistance, you are using your energy effectively and to its fullest potential. When you can direct this energy effectively, this energy manifests your desire.

The easiest and most efficient way to use magic is through the natural flow of the universe. One way this is accomplished is through alignment with the vibrational sequence of the seasons. This alignment brings the individual into contact with higher energy forms, such as those represented by the Gods and Goddesses of myth and legend. Gods and Goddesses are the masculine (positive pole) and feminine (negative pole) forces of the universe. They are known by many names in many different traditions and parts of the world. They are considered to be the communication link between humans and the "ALL" of Supreme Life Force.

By combining our energy with that of higher-plane forces, we create a circuit which allows us to give, as well as receive, energy. The energy that we can draw down from the higher planes, combined with our own personal energy, gives us the power to make magic work.

There are four major changes in the yearly cycle. These are spring, summer, fall, and winter. These are divided into four minor and more subtle seasonal changes. For those who are affiliated with Pagan Groves or other magical groups, these occasions are referred to as Sabbats or Great Days and they provide us with a time of celebration and thanksgiving.

These special times occur approximately every six weeks, beginning with Samhain on October 31st. To the magically inclined, these Sabbats are not just a change of season and weather, but are a reflection of the life cycle processes of birth, life, and death. Physically as well as spiritually, we express our understanding of these principles by making uses of these special times of power.

There are several ways of looking at these Great Days or Sabbats in connection with magic. One is through the classic myth regarding the union of the Lord of life and death with the Lady of birth and renewal. Another way is through the ballad, in which songs like "John Barley Corn" explain the cycle of life through a series of poetic verses. Probably the most uncomplicated way to explain these times of power is from the agricultural standpoint.

Using agriculture as our example, we view the seasons in terms of planning, planting, harvesting, and resting. In the early spring, the farmer will *plan* his/her crop and garden, preparing to *plant* by late spring and early summer. In the late summer and early fall, the farmer will *harvest* his/her crops. In the late fall through winter, all is allowed to *rest* and regenerate.

Though most of us are not farmers, and the closest we get to the actual crop is in the grocery store, we can still appreciate the farmer's simple and natural approach towards the work at hand. You never see a farmer out in his field in August planting a new crop. Even if he/she were able to get the seeds to germinate, the frost in six weeks would kill the small, delicate plants. Magic is the same—if we plan and plant the seeds of our desires at the appropriate times, then our wishes will surely manifest. On the other hand, if we attempt to work in opposition to the natural flow, then the rewards of our labors will be slim or nonexistent.

The first thing we need to do is take the seasons and break them down into eight segments. This shows us the sequence of vibrations in the universe. Knowing the vibrations, our actions can come into harmony with those of the universe. Once we begin to work with this natural vibrational frequency, magic becomes almost effortless. It seems as if time speeds up and what was just a dream a month ago is now a reality.

A good example of going with the flow is walking up the escalator which is moving in an upwards direction. You will certainly get to the top faster, and with less effort, than if you just stood there or used the stairs. By combining the power of the escalator with that of walking, you reach your destination sooner. However, if you try to walk down the up escalator, you will be going against the flow, it will take more time and effort, as well as create problems with the other passengers. It is only reasonable that if we go with the flow we will achieve success more quickly and with less opposition.

As we look to the seasonal Great Days or Sabbats, keep the example of the escalator in mind. We want to work with the flow of energy, rather than oppose it. When we combine our personal energy with that of nature, we automatically enhance everything we do.

The first step is to learn what the Great Days or Sabbats are all about, what they mean on a physical as well as spiritual plane. Once their meanings are clear, then we can begin to correlate their significance with our needs. The following outline briefly explains the application of each Sabbat, the relationship to both the physical and spiritual plane, and the corresponding symbolism.

The Sabbats or Great Days of Power

Yule or Winter Solstice, December 19–22: (*Think*) This is the time of year that you will begin to think about what you want to do in the coming year. This is when you will formulate ideas, organize your thoughts and decide what you wish to work towards. (Herbs, oils, and incense help to heighten awareness and should be used in offerings at this time.)

Imbolc, February 1: (*Prepare*) Now is when you will want to synthesize your ideas, map or chart out on paper in physical form what your goals are; choose a specific goal and direct your energy towards this.(Candles and lamps help to shed light on our desires; work with them at this time).

Vernal Equinox, March 19–22: (*Begin or Plant*) This is when you consummate the seeds of your desires by actually planting them. Here is the first physical step in the process, as you plant a seed which symbolically represents the outcome of your desire. (Seeds, bulbs and young plants are good to energize at this time with your aspirations and desires.)

Beltane or May Eve, April 30: (*Act or Movement*) Here we see the reaffirmation and union of energies, the movement toward the last half of the manifestation process. We have planted the seeds of desire, now we must reaffirm what we want as we energize the seeds. (Flowers, green plants and the abundance of nature remind us of what we are working for).

Summer Solstice, June 19–22: (*Nurture*) This is the time when the energies of polarity combine, as the opposites come into agreement. All effort at this time is put into the desired goal as we water our efforts with love and energy. (Water, fluid, and sacred oil remind us of our intentions and impending goal).

Lughnasadh, August 1: (*Accept*) Here we have the birth of our idea; our goal has begun to actually physically manifest and now we must assume responsibility for it. Just like the farmer who now has crops which he/she can begin to harvest, so too do we have the very beginnings of our goal in sight. (Corn, grain and loaves baked from the first harvest symbolize what is to come).

Autumnal Equinox, September 19–22: (*Receive*) At this point we should have that which we have been working for well within our reach. Technically, our goal has manifested by this time and we should be thankful for it and working to maintain it. (The corn baba serves as a representation of the goal and what we hope it will bring).

Samhain, October 31: (*Return*) Now is the time to release all negative thoughts and vibrations which may hinder the growth and progress of our manifested goal. This is the time to get rid of anything which may be holding us back. (Offerings of objects or petitions which represent or state what we want to get rid of).

As you look at the meaning of each Sabbat, a pattern appears. This pattern is one of a logical progression through each of the seasonal changes. When looked at separately, each one of these points in time is unique and special. However, when viewed collectively and in relation to each other, they provide the ideal situation for beginning and ending magical operations.

Magic and reclaiming personal power is merely a matter of combining what is at hand, or already exists, with the energy of a specific desire. When this is done, a special dynamic is created and the process of the manifestation cycle is completed. When I use the word "dynamic," I mean an energy state that is in the process of converting one thing into another. This may sound confusing, but in reality it is very simple. For once you begin to incorporate the natural energy of the universe into your daily life, magic becomes almost second nature. Things just seem to happen the way you want them to.

Most of what I am saying will become apparent as you read through each of the Sabbats rituals. They are like seasonal plays which recreate in symbolic form the journey through birth, life, and death. By focusing our energy on the Sabbats, we come into alignment with the seasonal vibrations of the universe. These vibrations or energies help to push our desires through their various stages of development. From planning through planting to harvest, we have the powers of nature working with us, adding strength and energy to our personal magical operations.

The Sabbats provide us with a natural time frame in which to work and measure our progress. In short, using the Sabbats as a formula for success is very simple. First, you *think* about what you want to do or accomplish at Yule; then write this down and make a talisman to represent the idea. At Imbolc, you will begin to *prepare* for the accomplishment of your goal. You will use a candle as your focal point. When the Spring Equinox arrives, it is time to actually *plant* the seeds of your desire. This is done by energizing and planting seeds that will grow, giving symbolic life in physical form to your goals. During Beltane and Summer Solstice, you will *nurture* both your plant and your desire with specially energized water. The water is symbolic of the life-giving and nurturing energy of the Earth Mother. By the time Lughnasadh has arrived, you should be ready to *accept* the responsibility for your goal by blessing the corn at the first harvest. By the Autumn Equinox, you should have *received* your desire and can then give thanks through the corn. Samhain is the time you will want to *return and release* any negativity which may surround your newly acquired objectives, so you can stabilize yourself and begin again with something new.

The Sabbat rituals which are presented in Chapter Eight are complete in their content. They are exactly the way we perform them in our circles at Our Lady of Enchantment. They are intended for group participation, but can be executed equally well by the individual. It may take slightly longer to do them solo, but as Sabbats are sacred times of great power, the extra effort is worth it.

I have limited my remarks and comments on the Sabbats so they can be followed easily, without interruption. Be sure to read through the Sabbat rituals several times. Rehearse them, especially when working with others. This always makes for a better ritual and helps in the formation of group bonding.

Important Ritual Information

There are several segments of the rituals which do not appear in the ritual text. These are:

(1) The Invocation to the Goddess.
(2) The Invocation to the God.
(3) The Rite of Union.

The reason for this is that these segments are lengthy and *should be memorized* for proper effect. These and other special invocations and rituals appear in their entirety in Appendix I.

Prior to each Sabbat ritual, all members should gather in an area away from the circle itself (if possible). During this time the leaders should go over the ritual, reading it aloud. If there are any questions they should be dealt with at this time. The middle of ritual is not the time for questions or doubts. At this time it is always a good idea to have a short seasonal reading or meditation to help set the mood. Classical or New Age music is always welcome and can aid in consciousness-raising both before and during the ceremony. Pre-ritual time is as important as the ritual itself. This is when the state of mind is set, helping to awaken the higher self to what follows.

CHAPTER NINE

The Celebration of Tradition

The Eight Sabbat Rituals

The Winter Solstice, Yule

Yule is a pre-Christian holiday or festival which is celebrated on the Winter Solstice around the 21st of December. It is the true New Year, both astronomically as well as spiritually. At this time we see the simultaneous death and rebirth of the Sun-God represented in the shortest day and longest night of the year. From this time forward the sun grows in power and strength.

To our ancestors, from whom our teachings come, fertility was an important aspect of daily life. As the sun is vital to the concept of growth and fertility, it is only natural that its return was celebrated with elaborate rituals and ceremonies. Though we don't necessarily use the Sabbat rites for fertility in a physical sense, the energy is still there and we can tap into it.

Yule is the time to *think* about what you want to accomplish in the months to come. Now is the time to outline the goals you wish to work towards. As the Sabbats progress, you will refine and narrow down these goals in content and purpose. The magical activity ap-

propriate for this time is the creation of a talisman which expresses your desires. Use seasonal items to create it. This talisman, along with a small burnable offering which reflects your desire, will be needed for the ceremony. For more information and suggestions on talismans and offerings see Chapter Ten and Appendix II.

A Ceremony for Yule

In preparation for this ritual you will need to cover your altar with a red cloth. Place the following items upon the altar: two red altar candles, a brazier or large incense burner, a chalice, an athame, a large red pillar candle on top of the pentacle, a bell, a bowl of salt, a bowl of water, and a sprig of holly tied with red and green ribbons. You will need to place a candle at each of the quadrants in the appropriate color. For the Rite of Union you will need hearty burgundy and a dry white wine or non-alcoholic alternatives. Other items needed are charcoal, matches and seasonal incense.

Each participant will want to bring their offering and talisman with them to the circle to be charged. When the ritual is over, members take their talismans with them.

Yule / Winter Solstice Ritual

(C) With a lighted taper, the Celebrant enters the ritual area and all follow, circumambulating three times, spiraling inward towards the altar. (C) The Celebrant places incense upon the coals and lights the altar candles, saying the following:

> (While lighting the right candle): *Blessed be the Fire of Faith which brings forth the Light.*

> (While lighting the left candle): *Blessed be the Light of the World which brings forth Life.*

(C) Now facing the altar, the Celebrant says:

Blessed be the White Goddess.
Blessed be the Sacrificed King.
Blessed be their Spiritual Seed.
Blessed be Cerridwen and Cernunnos.

(All)

Ayea, ayea, Cerridwen,
Ayea, ayea, Cerridwen,
Ayea, ayea, Cerridwen,
Ayea, ayea, ayea.

Ayea, ayea, Cernunnos,
Ayea, ayea, Cernunnos,
Ayea, ayea, Cernunnos,
Ayea, ayea, ayea.

(C) The Celebrant takes the sprig of holly, dips it into the water and then sprinkles it with salt. This is then used to cleanse the area by walking deosil (clockwise) around the circle and shaking the holly saying:

> *All negative thoughts are banished,*
> *All unwanted vibrations gone,*
> *Only the forces and powers we wish,*
> *Shall be with us from this moment on.*

(C) The Celebrant will now light the quadrant candles as follows, beginning in the East:

> (East) *Our Lady of the Whirling Winds, Host of the Rising Sun, Guardian of the Spirit of Light, be with us now.*

> (South) *Our Lord of Fire and Flame, Host of the Mid-Day Sun, Guardian of the Fires of Life, be with us now.*

> (West) *Our Lady of the Ocean and Tides, Host of the Setting Sun, Guardian of the Passions of Man, be with us now.*

> (North) *Our Lord of Mountains and Fields, Host of the Midnight Sun, Guardian of the Wisdom of the Ages, be with us now.*

(LF) The Lead Female will now consecrate the elements and cast the circle.

(LM) The Lead Male will now call upon the Guardians of the four quadrants, beginning in the East.

(LF) The Lead Female stands facing the altar and will now *invoke the Goddess*[1]

---

[1] The invocations to the the Goddess and the God are found in Appendix I.

(All)

> *Ayea, ayea, Cerridwen,*
> *Ayea, ayea, Cerridwen,*
> *Ayea, ayea, Cerridwen,*
> *Ayea, ayea, ayea.*

(C) The Celebrant comes forward and addresses the group as follows:

> *Desolate and dormant is the Earth above,*
> *Fertile and vital is its Soul below.*
> *Our mind knows what our eyes cannot see,*
> *For all is resting and waiting.*
> *The canopy of Death hangs heavy about us,*
> *Life ends and Life begins all in a moment.*
> *We attain spiritual strength and happiness*
> *When we seek from within rather than from without.*
> *Now we welcome back our Lord of Life and Death,*
> *And the beauty of birth and renewal.*

(LM) The Lead Male stands facing the altar and invokes the God.

(All)

> *Ayea, ayea, Cernunnos,*
> *Ayea, ayea, Cernunnos,*
> *ayea, ayea, Cernunnos,*
> *Ayea, ayea, ayea.*

(C) The Celebrant comes forward, lights the yellow or gold working candle to welcome back the light, and says:

Lord and Lady of the Night,
Of mist and of moonlight,
Though you are seldom seen
We meet you in heart, mind and dream.
Bless now our thoughts, works and deeds,
That they shall fulfill our wishes and needs.
On this night we honor thee
To make our desires a reality,
Our energy we now give to thee
For your blessings, so shall it be.

(C) The Celebrant hands the candle to another member of the group who will then offer it at each of the quadrants as follows, beginning in the East:

(East) *Blessed be the Light coming from the East, which inspires us.*

(South) *Blessed be the Fire coming from the South, which warms us.*

(West) *Blessed be the Moisture coming from the West, which cools us.*

(North) *Blessed be the Fertile Earth of the North, which provides for us.*

The candle is now placed on the pentacle in the center of the altar.

(LF) The Lead Female will now address the group as follows:

For now the time has come for each to consider what he or she will work toward in the months to come.

What we put into motion this night will be our reward at the harvest.

Our Lord and Lady remind us to ask only for what we need and we will ever abound.

Let us now unite in perfect love and perfect trust, as we welcome back our Lord of Light and Life.

All members now place their talismans in the center of the circle (around or on the altar if possible). One by one they will then come forward. They will make their wish, and then carefully set fire to their offering, placing it in the incense burner or brazier. As the smoke rises up, carrying the wishes to the Gods, all take hands and chant.

God of Glory
God of Light
Bless us all
On Solstice Night.

All members take a moment to reflect when the chant is finished. The chant raises energy which is transferred to the talismans.

(LF) The Lead Female and (LM) Lead Male will now do the *Rite of Union*. (The Rite of Union is symbolic of the union or sacred marriage of the God and Goddess, the feminine and masculine forces of nature, coming together to unite and become one.) The wine is then passed. Each person says "Perfect Love and Perfect Trust" as they receive and then pass on the cup.

(LM) The Lead Male will now address the group as follows:

On this night we have welcomed back our Lord of Light and our Lady of Life.

May all those seeking their wonderment and illumination be guided by our torches.

Let all those gathered here in their honor take a measure of their Strength, Power and Wisdom home. All hail to Cerridwen and Cernunnos.

(All)

Ayea, ayea, Cerridwen
Ayea, ayea, Cerridwen
Ayea, ayea, Cerridwen
Ayea, ayea, ayea.

Ayea, ayea, Cernunnos
Ayea, ayea, Cernunnos
Ayea, ayea, Cernunnos
Ayea, ayea, ayea.

(C) The Celebrant will now extinguish the quadrant candles, beginning in the North and proceeding widdershins (counter-clockwise) saying:

(North) *Our Lord of Mountains and Fields, Host of the Midnight Sun, Guardian of the Wisdom of the Ages, we thank thee for thy blessings.*

(West) *Our Lady of the Ocean Tides, Host of the Setting Sun, Guardian of the Passions of Man, we thank thee for thy blessings.*

(South) *Our Lord of Fire and Flame, Host of the Mid-Day Sun, Guardian of the Fires of Life, we thank thee for thy blessings.*

(East) *Our Lady of the Whirling Winds, Host of the Rising Sun, Guardian of the Spirit of Light, we thank thee for thy blessings.*

(LM) The Lead Male will now dismiss the Guardians. Beginning in the North and proceeding in a widdershins (counter-clockwise) manner to the West.

(LF) The Lead Female will now banish the circle, moving in a widdershins manner.

The Rite is ended.

Personal Note:
In most Wiccan or magical groups it is traditional to have a feast following an important ceremony. This helps to ground the energy of the participants, as well as bringing members together in a social sense. The most practical way to do this is to make a list of foods you wish to serve and then have each member bring something from the list.

Imbolc / Oimele

Imbolc, also known as Oimele or Brigantia, is celebrated on February 1st. This is the feast of the waxing light or feast of lights, and is ascribed to the Goddess Bridget or Bride. This Great Day is associated with the coming again of life and light. Imbolc marks the awakening of the earth and the promise of spring; it is definitely a time of new beginnings.

In Greece, during the Eleusinian Mysteries, people held a torch light procession on February 1st in honor of Demeter. The torch light was to aid her in her search for her lost daughter Persephone. When she was found, light returned to the world. This is also the time when the young lord God courted the virgin-maiden aspect of the

Goddess. Their passion for each other is felt in the seasonal energy at this time. Closely related to Imbolc is the Christian festival of Candlemas, which is celebrated on February 2nd and is a time of purification.

Now is when you want to *prepare* for what you wish to accomplish in the months to come. You should use this time to clarify and refine what you began at Yule. As this is a festival of lights, you will use candles whose color, size and shape best reflect your goal. These will be brought to the circle and energized during the ritual. When taken home and burned daily, the candles will reaffirm and reflect the energy of their intended desire. See Appendix II for candle correspondences and burning time frames.

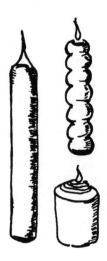

A Ceremony for Imbolc

In preparation for this ceremony, cover the altar with a white cloth. Place the following upon the altar: two pink or white altar candles, an incense burner, a chalice, an athame, a bell, a pentacle, and salt and water bowls. There should be a vase of delicate, small, fresh flowers, such as pink rose buds and babies breath. There should also be a large white or pink "working" candle, in addition to the altar candles. For wine, use white and pink Chablis. Candles of the proper color are placed at each of the quadrants. You will also need charcoal, matches, and some seasonal incense.

Each participant will want to bring a candle which corresponds to what they are working for. These candles will be energized during the ritual.

Imbolc / Oimele Ritual

All participants wait outside the circle area.

(C) The Celebrant enters the circle, circumambulates three times deosil (clockwise), stops before the altar, bows or genuflects, and tones the bell three times. He or she then places incense upon the coals and lights the altar candles saying:

> (While lighting the right candle): *Gallant Lord, Protector and Father of all, Bring forth Light, Life and Wisdom.*

> (While lighting the left candle): *White Maiden, Gentle Mother, Silent One, Deliver us from Ignorance and Darkness.*

(C) The Celebrant tones the bell three more times, places more incense upon the coals, and lights the quadrant candles as follows:

> (East) *I light the East to bring forth the Dawn and the Spirit of Light.*

> (South) *I light the South to bring forth the Power and Spirit of Life.*

> (West) *I light the West to bring forth the Passion and Spirit of Love.*

> (North) *I light the North to bring forth the Balance and the Spirit of Wisdom.*

All members enter the circle area, circumambulate three times while chanting:

(All)

Out of Death comes Life,
Out of Darkness comes Light,
Out of Winter comes Spring.

(C) The Celebrant tones the bell three times and says the following:

Our Lady has been with us from the beginning,
She is ever our Light and Life.
Our Lord has been with us from the beginning,
He is ever our Strength and Power.

(LF) The Lead Female will now consecrate the elements and cast the circle.

(LM) The Lead Male will now call upon the Guardians of the four quadrants.

(LM) The Lead Male speaks to the group as follows:

The Sun has been reborn and our Lord has risen,
The Moon reflects his glory and our Lady is transformed.
Together they bring forth Light, Life and Love, Delivering us from Darkness, Death and Sorrow.
Out of Death comes Life,
Out of Darkness comes Light,
Out of Winter comes Spring.

(All)

Out of Death comes Life,
Out of Darkness comes Light,
Out of Winter comes Spring.

(LF) The Lead Female stands before the altar and *invokes the Goddess.*

(All)

> *Ayea, ayea, Cerridwen*
> *Ayea, ayea, Cerridwen*
> *Ayea, ayea, Cerridwen*
> *Ayea, ayea, ayea.*

(C) The Celebrant will now come forward and light the working candle saying:

> *Let us banish the Winter and welcome the Spring,*
> *As Light brings life to every living thing.*
> *The Glory of the Gods we now behold,*
> *For all that is given returns three-fold.*
> *As we revel in the warmth of their presence and light,*
> *We pray they will grant our needs and wishes this night.*
>
> *For out of Death comes Life,*
> *Out of Darkness comes Light,*
> *Out of Winter comes Spring.*

(All)

> *Out of Death comes Life,*
> *Out of Darkness comes Light,*
> *Out of Winter comes Spring.*

(LM) The Lead Male stands before the altar and *invokes the God.*

(All)

> *Ayea, ayea, Cernunnos*
> *Ayea, ayea, Cernunnos*
> *Ayea, ayea, Cernunnos*
> *Ayea, ayea, ayea.*

(LM) The Lead Male places incense upon the coals and address the group as follows:

> *On this night as we approach new beginnings,*
> *Now do we pledge ourselves to the Goddess.*
> *On this night as we feel the Life Force within,*
> *Now do we pledge ourselves to the God.*
> *On this night as we realize our potential,*
> *Now do we pledge ourselves to Spiritual Growth.*

Each participant will come forward one at a time, kneel before the altar and petition the God/Goddess to grant their wishes. Each person will place his or her candle on the floor or altar (if there is room) and then step back into place.

(LF) The Lead Female speaks the following part and then steps back into the circle:

> *Our Lord, Mighty Ruler of the Solar Orb,*
> *Approaches now with lusty anticipation.*
> *The Flames of Passion have been aroused*
> *And his Seed of Life brings renewal.*

(LM) The Lead Male speaks the following part and then steps back into the circle:

> *Our Lady, White Maiden, Enchantress,*
> *Brings us Life and Light.*
> *She is the inspiration behind all creation.*
> *This night she transforms Death into Life.*

(C) The Celebrant speaks the following part, steps back into the circle, and asks everyone to take hands:

> *Our Lady is Bridget, Goddess of Fire,*
> *Hearth, Home and Desire.*

She forms the Passion in our great God's heart
So that within her, the Seed of Life he shall impart.
Now Bridget is our Queen of Spring,
Bringing forth beauty to every living thing.

All members continue to hold hands while chanting the following to energize the candles:

Passion and fire,
Bring forth desire.

(LM) and (LF) will now do the *Rite of Union*. The wine is passed and each answers "In Perfect Love and Perfect Trust."

(LF) The Lead Female faces the altar and addresses the God and Goddess as follows:

Lady of Light, Mother of Darkness, Wise One,
Thou art pure in spirit, transcendent, and full of
eternal love.
Lord of Fire, Father of Light, Passionate One, Thou
art our protector, triumphant warrior, and king.
Be now your blessings upon all this night; so shall
it be.

(C) The Celebrant extinguishes the quadrant candles, beginning in the North, proceeding in a widdershins manner (counter-clockwise), saying:

(North) *Let the Spirit of Balance and Wisdom be with all.*

(West) *Let the Spirit of Passion and Love be with all.*

(South) *Let the Spirit of Power and Life be with all.*

(East) *Let the Spirit of the Dawn and Light be with all.*

(LM) The Lead Male dismisses the Guardians in a widdershins manner, beginning in the North.

(LF) The Lead Female banishes the circle in a widdershins manner.

The Rite is ended.

The Spring Equinox, Ostara

The Spring (or Vernal) Equinox is celebrated around the 21st of March. This is the time when the sun crosses the plane of the equator, making the day and night of equal length. Equinox is the actual beginning of spring and the agricultural season. We see many of the Christian Easter customs coming from this festive occasion. The most popular of these practices is that of decorating eggs. In ancient Egypt, Rome, Greece and Persia, brightly colored eggs were eaten at this time as symbolic of immortality, fertility and resurrection.

The Equinox is a time of balance, when we seek equality and harmony between the masculine and feminine forces in nature. This is also the time when we physically as well as symbolically plant the seeds of our desires. The seeds which will grow into plants represent what we are working for. When the plant bears fruit at harvest, so too should our desire manifest in physical form.

Each participant brings seeds which symbolize their desire. The seeds can be placed in pouches, plastic eggs, or left in their packets and tied with colorful ribbon. I suggest choosing several different kinds of seeds to represent different aspects of your desire. Using a job promotion as an example, you might want seeds for communication, some for prosperity and another kind for success.

Remember, what you decided to do at Yule and put into motion at Imbolc, you will be planting both physically and spiritually tonight.

A Ceremony for the Spring Equinox

In preparation for this ritual, cover your altar with a pastel, lavender cloth and upon it place two lavender altar candles. There should be vases of fresh flowers, a bell, the athame, the chalice, an incense burner and two bowls for the salt and water. A large lavender working candle is needed, as well as charcoal, incense, and fruity red and white wines. Candles are placed at each of the quadrants in their respective colors.

Each participant will want to bring their seeds with them into ritual for energizing and blessing. They will then take these home and plant them. The physical plants serve to remind us of our goals.

Vernal Equinox / Ostara Ritual
(All) All of the members gather in the ritual area around the altar.

(C) The celebrant tones the bell three times and says the following:

Holy art thou, Lady of the Universe.
Holy art thou, Lord of all Creation.
Be thou with us this night in Life and Spirit.

(C) The Celebrant lights the altar candles saying:

(While lighting the right candle): *Lord of the Dark Realm descend,*
And move the spirit of our soul.
Renew within the vital force,
Blend thy energies, make us whole.

(While lighting the left candle): *Lady from the Dark Realm come, lead us into the new dawning day,*
Protect us from the passions of man,
Guide us along thy secret way.

(C) The Celebrant tones the bell three times, places incense on the coals, and lights the quadrant candles as follows:

(East) *Blessed be the Air of the Eternal Spirit,*
For it brings forth new beginnings.

(South) *Blessed be the Fire of Passion,*
For it gives us protection and power.

(West) *Blessed be the Waters of Regeneration,*
For they render rest and renewal.

(North) *Blessed be the Earth of Remembrance,*
For it provides hope and promise.

(LF) The Lead Female will now tone the bell three times, consecrate the elements and cast the circle.

(LM) The Lead Male will now call upon the Guardians of the four quadrants.

(LM) The Lead Male addresses the group as follows:

> *Our Lord and Lady are known by many names;*
> *They are our light and life.*
> *We stand within their sacred temple and*
> *Feel their presence, passion and power.*
> *This is their house, their time, their season.*
> *All hail to thee Cerridwen and Cernunnos.*

(All)

> *Ayea, ayea, Cerridwen*
> *Ayea, ayea, Cerridwen*
> *Ayea, ayea, Cerridwen*
> *Ayea, ayea, ayea.*
>
> *Ayea, ayea, Cernunnos*
> *Ayea, ayea, Cernunnos*
> *Ayea, ayea, Cernunnos*
> *Ayea, ayea, ayea.*

(LF) The Lead Female will now do the *invocation to the Goddess.*

(All)

> *Ayea, ayea, Cerridwen*
> *Ayea, ayea, Cerridwen*
> *Ayea, ayea, Cerridwen*
> *Ayea, ayea, ayea.*

(LM) The Lead Male will now do *the invocation to the God.*

(All)

> *Ayea, ayea, Cernunnos*
> *Ayea, ayea, Cernunnos*

Ayea, ayea, Cernunnos
Ayea, ayea, ayea.

(C) The Celebrant will now light the yellow working candle, saying:

Our Lord and Lady of Heaven and Earth,
To Life and Spring now give birth.
At this time of equal night and equal light
To you, we pray, banish Winter's plight.

(C) The Celebrant now hands the candle to another celebrant who will offer it at each of the quadrants as follows:

(East) *Let now the Spirit of Light be with us,*
for inspiration and imagination.

(South) *Let now the Spirit of Life be with us,*
for strength and power.

(West) *Let now the Spirit of Love be with us,*
for compassion and understanding.

(North) *Let now the Spirit of Wisdom be with us,*
for perception and knowledge.

(C) The Celebrant now places the candle on the pentacle in the center of the altar. Each member comes forward and places his or her seeds on the floor or if there is room on the altar. They all step back, forming a circle and holding hands while chanting the following to direct the energy into the seeds:

Blessed be the seeds
that satisfy our needs.

(LM) and (LF) will now do the *Rite of Union* and all partake of the wine in Perfect Love and Perfect Trust.

(LF) The Lead Female faces the altar, saying the following:

> *Hail to thee Cerridwen and Cernunnos,*
> *For you are our light and life.*
> *We pray for your blessings and guidance,*
> *Keep us steadfast upon your path of intelligence.*
> *For as your awakened land blossoms forth,*
> *So shall we bring honor and glory to your name.*

(All)

> *Ayea, ayea, Cerridwen*
> *Ayea, ayea, Cerridwen*
> *Ayea, ayea, Cerridwen*
> *Ayea, ayea, ayea.*
>
> *Ayea, ayea, Cernunnos*
> *Ayea, ayea, Cernunnos*
> *Ayea, ayea, Cernunnos*
> *Ayea, ayea, ayea.*

(C) The Celebrant will now come forward, tone the bell three times and then extinguish the quadrant candles beginning in the North:

> (North) *Let us always remember the Earth, for it provides us with hope and promise.*
>
> (West) *Let us always remember the Waters of Regeneration, for they render rest and renewal.*
>
> (South) *Let us always remember the Fires of Passion, for they give us protection and power.*

(East) *Let us always remember the Eternal Spirit,*
for it brings forth new beginnings.

(LM) The Lead Male will now dismiss the Guardians, beginning in the North and proceeding widdershins (counter-clockwise).

(LF) The Lead Female will now banish the circle in a widdershins manner.

Beltane / May Eve

Beltane is celebrated on April 30th, (May Eve) and is primarily a fire and fertility festival. Beltane, meaning "Bel-Fire," is derived from the Celtic God Bel, also known as Beli or Balor, which simply means Lord. Some seem to think that Bel was comparable to the Celtic Gaul God, Cernunnos. This is possible, as most male Gods relate to the sun and fire aspects.

Beltane is also the time of the May Queen, in which a young woman was chosen from the village to represent the Earth Goddess and reflected the transformation of maiden to mother. This was also the time of the kindling of the "Need Fire," when all fires in the village were extinguished and then ritually relit the following day.

Fertility played an important role in the Beltane celebrations. The most significant symbol of this was the May Pole, also known as the *axis mundi,* around which the universe revolved. The pole personified the thrusting masculine force, and the disk at the top depicted the receptive female. There were seven colored ribbons tied to it, and they represented the seven colors of the rainbow. Fire and fertility, for the most part, dominated the rituals at this time.

On this night, we spiritually welcome back the Goddess in the form of the May Queen, and begin to *actively* pursue our goals on the material plane. Now is the time to take action and physically put effort into your goals. Using a job promotion as an example, now would be the time to make your desires known to your supervisors. Let them see that you are both interested and capable of assuming more responsibility.

For this ceremony, you will need your personal working wand, a flower which represents your goal and some green ribbon. Tie the flower to your wand and bring it with you to ritual.

A Ceremony for Beltane

In preparation for this ritual, cover your altar with a green cloth and place two green altar candles upon it. There should be two vases filled with fresh flowers and a crown of fresh flowers to place on the head of the Lead Female (LF), who will represent the May Queen. Also needed are the chalice, athame, bell, pentacle, salt and water bowls, a large green working candle, an incense burner, red and white wine, a sweet-flowery incense, charcoal, and matches. (May wine is a nice substitute for the white wine. It is made by taking fresh woodruff, bruising it and placing it in a bottle of light white wine, such as Chablis or Mountain Rhine. The longer it sits, the better it gets.)

Each participant will bring his or her working wand. It should be decorated with a flower and green ribbon. Once energized with the seasonal vibration, the wands will serve to direct energy towards the desired goals.

Beltane / May Eve Ritual

(C) The Celebrant enters the circle carrying the working candle, two participants follow with lighted tapers and circumambulate three times. They stop at the altar and the Celebrant (C), tones the bell three times. The rest of the group enters the circle except for the Lead Female (LF).

(C) The Celebrant now places some incense upon the coals and the two participants light the altar candles, first the participant on the right (R) and then the participant on the left (L) as they say:

> (R) *Blessed be our Lord of Light and Power,*
> *He transforms our souls for this hour.*
>
> (L) *Blessed be our Lady of Love and Passion,*
> *For our hearts and future she shall fashion.*

(C) The Celebrant faces the altar, tones the bell three times and says the following:

> *Let now the Light and Life of the Creative Spirit,*
> *Deliver us from Darkness, bring us Wisdom and*
> *Clear Vision, as we progress towards our Lord and*
> *Lady. So be it.*

(C) The Celebrant tones the bell three times and will then light the quadrant candles as follows:

> (East) *I bring Light to the East, the home of the*
> *Eternal Spirit.*

(South) *I bring Light to the South, the home of the Divine Spark.*

(West) *I bring Light to the West, the home of the Final Atonement.*

(North) *I bring Light to the North, the home of All Creation.*

(LM) The Lead Male lights the working candle saying:

> *By this Light do I bring blessings from the Dawn of Time. As it was then, so it shall be now, according to the ways of the Wise Ones. Time decrees that our Lord and Ruler of the Mystic Realm, Guardian of the Underworld, Divine King, shall take his leave, for this be the time of Light and Life.*

(LM) The Lead Male will now do the *invocation of the God.*

(All)

> *Ayea, ayea, Cernunnos*
> *Ayea, ayea, Cernunnos*
> *Ayea, ayea, Cernunnos*
> *Ayea, ayea, ayea.*

(LM) The Lead Male will now go to the edge of the circle, carrying the lighted candle. He welcomes the Lady (LF) to the circle saying:

> *All homage to thee, Lady of the summer Sun, Thou who brings Life and Light to all. On this your most sacred of all nights, do I bid thee welcome.*
> *I pray, Great Mother, deliver us from darkness and breathe new life into our hearts, minds and souls.*

(LM) With the candle, the Lead Male now leads the way to the altar and then places the candle upon the pentacle.

(LF) The Lead Female will now consecrate the elements and cast the circle.

(LM) The Lead Male will now call upon the Guardians of the four quadrants.

(LF) The Lead Female addresses the group as follows:

> *Cerridwen, Glorious Lady of the Moon, Holiest of Holy, we honor thee this night. Thou art Maiden, Mother, Crone, Transcendent, Ageless Splendor, to whom we pay homage. Now do we celebrate the cycle, the return, the promise. For all that shall be touched by thy Light, shall be transformed.*

(All)

> *Ayea, ayea, Cerridwen*
> *Ayea, ayea. Cerridwen*
> *Ayea, ayea, Cerridwen*
> *Ayea, ayea, ayea.*

(C) The Celebrant tones the bells three times, places incense on the coals, picks up the working candle in offering and says the following:

> *We pray, Glorious Goddess of the Moon,*
> *As we stand between Day and Night,*
> *Your heavenly presence be with us soon,*
> *As Darkness gives way to the Light.*

(All)

Ayea, ayea, Cerridwen
Ayea, ayea, Cerridwen
Ayea, ayea, Cerridwen
Ayea, ayea, ayea.

(LM) The Lead Male now picks up the crown of flowers; the Lead Female (LF) kneels in front of him. He places the crown upon her head as he says the following:

Thou who rises from the Raging Sea,
Shall now accept thy destiny.
Let now the Lady of Inner Earth
To the land of promise give birth,
So that all the seed, fruit and grain
Shall in abundance come forth again.

(LF) The Lead Female rises, and does *the invocation to the Goddess.*

(All)

Ayea, ayea, Cerridwen
Ayea, ayea, Cerridwen
Ayea, ayea, Cerridwen
Ayea, ayea, ayea.

(LM) Address the group as follows:

Our Lady has been called by many names,
For She is the whole of all Life.
The Lord is the Divine Victim,
And He brings forth Hope.
Our Lord and Lady were of old
Worshipped in secret by those of wise faith.
In darkest forest or in humble hut
Were their names called out and
Blessings were brought forth.

Our Gods have been with us from the beginning;
They are the promise of Life Everlasting,
And at the end of desire is their mystery revealed.
Our Lord and Lady teach us that what so-ever we
Shall seek and not find within,
We shall never find without.
For thou art God and thou art Goddess,
And all are one in the eyes of the Mighty Ones.

(C) The Celebrant will now instruct the members to come forward one at a time and ask for what they want, as they place their wand on the altar. When each person is finished, they step back into the circle. All then take hands and raise the power by chanting the following:

Lovely Lady of the Moon,
Grant our needs and wishes soon.

The Lead Male (LM) and Lead Female (LF) will now do *the Rite of Union* to bless the wine. All will partake in Perfect Love and Perfect Trust.

(C) The Celebrant will tone the bells three times and address the group as follows:

Blessed is this time of Enlightenment.
Our seeds have been sown and our labors
Shall be rewarded.
For as our precious plants grow strong,
So too shall the rewards of the spirit
Be brought to fulfillment.
Let us always remember to give as we receive,
For we are all Children of the Goddess.

(C) The Celebrant will now extinguish the quadrant candles as follows:

(North) *Let now the home of all Creation bless us with abundance.*

(West) *Let now the home of the Final Atonement bless us with wisdom.*

(South) *Let now the home of the Divine Spark bless us with energy and power.*

(East) *Let now the home of the Eternal Spirit bless us with inspiration and insight.*

(LM) The Lead Male will now dismiss the Guardians of the four quadrants, proceeding in a widdershins (counter-clockwise) manner.

(LF) The Lead Female will now banish the circle in a widdershins manner.

The Rite is ended.

The Summer Solstice / Midsummer

Midsummer or Summer Solstice is celebrated around the 21st of June and is the longest day and shortest night of the year. The festival of the Summer Solstice is concerned with both fire and water. As from this point onward the sun will decline in its power, the symbology of fire was used in keeping the sun alive. The water element was used for the ritual blessing of individuals, sacred wells, and springs.

One of the customs of our ancestors was leaping over or passing through fires. It was believed that the higher they jumped the higher the crops would grow. As with Beltane, cattle were driven through the fires for purification and fumigation. It was also believed that the fire repelled the powers of evil and would protect the cattle as well as all who passed through it.

Another symbol used at this time was the wheel. The turning of the wheel suggested the turning or progression of the seasons. Wheels were decorated with flowers and then lighted candles were placed on them. These were then taken to a body of water and set afloat.

From a symbolic and ritual standpoint, now is the time to *nurture* your goals or efforts. That which you have been working for should now be within range. You will want to continue to care for and sustain your impending goal in every possible way. Now is not the time to get careless or sloppy. On the other hand, being pushy or aggressive won't help either. Balance and steadfastness are the keys to success during Midsummer.

Midsummer or Summer Solstice is celebrated around the 21st of June and is the longest day and shortest night of the year. The festival of the Summer Solstice is concerned with both fire and water. As from this point onward the sun will decline in its power, the symbology of fire was used in keeping the sun alive. The water element was used for the ritual blessing of individuals, sacred wells and springs.

Because Midsummer is a celebration of both fire and water, you will need to make a *water candle*. This is accomplished by placing a short taper candle (the color of your desire) in a glass jar. Place this jar inside of another jar filled with water, food coloring, and a sprinkling of appropriate herbs (to give the water extra energy). The water will be used to water the plant which is growing from the seeds you planted at Spring Equinox.

A Ceremony for the Summer Solstice

In preparation for this ritual, cover your altar with a yellow cloth. Place upon the altar two yellow candles, the chalice, athame, incense burner, bell, and pentacle. Get a small cauldron or bowl, fill it with water and place a yellow floating candle in it (or substitute a water candle). Also needed are candles for the quadrants, some charcoal, incense, matches, and fresh flowers. Use a sweet, fruity red and white wine for the Rite of Union.

All those participating in the ritual will want to bring their water candles to the circle for energizing.

Summer Solstice/Midsummer Ritual

(LF), (LM) The Lead Female and Lead Male enter the circle area carrying lighted tapers.

(C) The Celebrant and other participants follow. All circumambulate three times, stopping at altar.

(C) The Celebrant tones the bell three times, places incense upon the coals, and says the following:

> *Blessed be our Lord and Lady,*
> *For they are our life and light.*
> *Blessed are they who walk the path,*
> *And all who are gathered here this night.*

(LM) The Lead Male will now light the right (R) altar candle saying:

> (R) *Cernunnos, be with us in truth and might,*
> *As in your honor this candle we light.*

(LF) The Lead Female will now light the left (L) altar candle saying:

(L) *Cerridwen, now send your divine guiding power,*
Through candle flame bless each this hour.

(C) The Celebrant will now light the quadrant candles as follows:

(East) *Let the winds of consciousness bring forth insight and wisdom, as the East gives rise to the light.*

(South) *Let the fires of awareness bring forth motivation and inspiration, as the South gives host to the sun.*

(West) *Let the waves of completeness bring forth love and passion, as the West accepts the twilight.*

(North) *Let the blossoming fertile Earth bring forth manifestation of desire, as the North returns from darkness.*

(LF) The Lead Female will now consecrate the elements and cast the circle.

(LM) The Lead Male will now call upon the Guardians of the four quadrants.

(C) The Celebrant will now tone the bell three times, lighting the floating candle while saying:

Our Lord is the Fire of the Golden Sphere,
Our Lady's time is now and she draws near,
For through the candle flame they speak,
Bringing insight and wisdom to all who seek,
To understand the mystery.
Within their knowledge lies
The secret to the key that will allow mankind to rise
Above the limitations of this confined Earth.

*To all we know and all we see: they have given
birth.*

(All)

*Ayea, ayea, Cerridwen
Ayea, ayea, Cerridwen
Ayea, ayea, Cerridwen
Ayea, ayea, ayea.*

*Ayea, ayea, Cernunnos
Ayea, ayea, Cernunnos
Ayea, ayea, Cernunnos
Ayea, ayea, ayea.*

(C) The Celebrant picks up the cauldron (bowl) with
the floating candle in it and proceeds to offer it at each of
the quadrants as follows:

(East) *The Sun shall rise and speak unto our spirits.*

(South) *The Sun shall radiate its power about us.*

(West) *The Sun shall set the mysteries in motion.*

(North) *The Sun shall manifest what has been
proven worthy.*

(C) The Celebrant now places the floating candle
back on the altar.

(LF) The Lead Female will now do the *invocation to
the Goddess.*

(All)

Ayea, ayea, Cerridwen
Ayea, ayea, Cerridwen
Ayea, ayea, Cerridwen
Ayea, ayea, ayea.

(LM) The Lead Male will now do the *invocation to the God.*

(All)

Ayea, ayea, Cernunnos
Ayea, ayea, Cernunnos
Ayea, ayea, Cernunnos
Ayea, ayea, ayea.

(LF) The Lead Female now addresses the group as follows:

At this time of light and life,
Do we celebrate the Summer Solstice.
For all life has blossomed forth,
And nature flourishes around us.
Great indeed is our joy this night,
As our Lord and Lady bless us with
their abundance.
Our Lord provides strength and passion, and our
Lady love and understanding.
They allow us to progress and grow,
And free us from past restrictions.
Great indeed are their blessings.

(All)

Ayea, ayea, Cerridwen
Ayea, ayea, Cerridwen
Ayea, ayea, Cerridwen
Ayea, ayea, ayea.

Ayea, ayea, Cernunnos
Ayea, ayea, Cernunnos
Ayea, ayea, Cernunnos
Ayea, ayea, ayea.

One at a time, all participants will bring their water candle to the altar, kneel and ask for what they wish. The candles are then placed around the altar on the floor. All take hands and chant the following in order to raise the power that is to be directed into the candles:

Sun and Flame
Bring joy and gain.

(LM) and (LF) The Lead Male and Lead Female will now bless the wine through the Rite of Union, all partake in Perfect Love and Perfect Trust.

(LM) The Lead Male faces the altar and says the following:

To the Lord and Lady,
Our gratitude we show,
As in life and spirit
We progress and grow.
Let us thank them
By our work and deed,
That we all may receive
What we wish and need.

(All)

Ayea, ayea, Cerridwen
Ayea, ayea, Cerridwen
Ayea, ayea, Cerridwen
Ayea, ayea, ayea.

Ayea, ayea, Cernunnos
Ayea, ayea, Cernunnos
Ayea, ayea, Cernunnos
Ayea, ayea, ayea.

(C) The Celebrant tones the bell three times and will extinguish the quadrant candles as follows:

(North) *Let now our desires manifest upon the fertile Earth, as the North returns to darkness.*

(West) *Let now our love and passion bring us feelings of completeness, as the West accepts the twilight.*

(South) *Let now the fires of awareness motivate us to action, as the South gives host to the Sun.*

(East) *Let the winds of consciousness provide us with insight and wisdom, as the east gives rise to the light.*

(LM) The Lead Male will now dismiss the Guardians of the four quadrants.

(LF) The Lead Female will now banish the circle.
The Rite Is ended.

Lughnasadh / Lammas

Lughnasadh (Celtic), or Lammas (Christian), is held on August 1st. Lughnasadh means *half-maes* or loaf feast and refers to the first loaves baked from the first grain harvested. These loaves were blessed by the priesthood and distributed among the members of the congregation. Observing this festival ensured an abundance of fruit and grain for the months to come. The first fruit picked or sheaf cut was considered to be sacred to the Gods and therefore treated in a special manner.

Corn and grain are the predominate features of rituals at this time because they symbolize the fertility of the earth, the awakening of life, and life coming from death. The golden ears of corn are seen as the offspring of the marriage of the sun and virgin earth. Corn and wine, like bread and wine, represent humankind's labor and ability to sustain life.

Wine and candle making were also important features of this time of year, along with food-preserving and other preparations for winter. Some customs include rush-bearing, decorating water wells with vines, and the blessing of food.

This is the first harvest and the time we *accept* the responsibility as well as rewards for our labors. At this time our goals should be in the early stages of physical manifestation. Continuing with our example of the job promotion, at this time you should be in training for your new position. You may not have the title yet, but you definitely have the promotion. The other benefits will follow.

For this ritual you will be blessing corn. This symbolizes your ability to produce results. It will also ensure the satisfactory completion of your work, or bountiful harvest, at the Autumn Equinox. All those participating in the ritual will want to bring three ears of fresh corn with them. These will be tied in bundles of three and blessed during the ceremony. This blessed corn will be taken home by members, dried, and then fashioned into a corn baba for the Autumn Equinox ceremony.

Another feature of this ritual is the blessing of John Barleycorn. John Barleycorn is a figure of a man, shaped out of a cookie dough. The dough contains both corn meal and barley flour. The ballad of John Barleycorn is very fitting for this time of year, as it repeats and enhances the theme of birth and life, death and return, in poetic form. (The recipe for John Barleycorn is in Appendix II).

A Ceremony for Lughnasadh

In preparation for this ritual, cover the altar with an orange cloth and place two gold-colored altar candles upon it. You will need the chalice, incense burner, bell, pentacle, athame, John Barleycorn, and a small bundle of corn tied with orange and gold ribbon. At each of the quadrants place the appropriate color candle and an ear of corn. Dry red and white wine are needed, as well as anointing oil, charcoal, seasonal incense, and matches.

Each participant will bring his or her corn bundle with them when they enter the circle.

Lughnasadh / Lammas Ritual

(LF) and (LM) The Lead Female and Lead Male enter the circle first and will anoint each member (male to female) as they enter. (They anoint the forehead with oil by tracing a pentagram on it and saying: "Blessed Be in the name of Cerridwen and Cernunnos.") When they have finished, they leave the circle to get the corn and John Barleycorn, which will eventually be placed upon the altar.

(C) The Celebrant will now light the altar candles saying:

(While lighting the right candle) *Our Lord is
the passion,
He brings forth the light;
The harvest is of his seed.*

(While lighting the left candle) *Our Lady is the
power,
She brings forth the life;
The harvest is her reward.*

(LF) and (LM) The Lead Female and Lead Male return to the circle, carrying the corn and John Barleycorn, circumambulating three times. They chant the following and all participants join in:

(All)

As the corn, we are reborn.

(C) The Celebrant and another participant will light the quadrant candles. As the Celebrant lights the candles, the participant will hold up the corn and say the following, beginning in the East:

(East) *I call upon soft and whispering winds,
The realm of intellect and perception
Bring forth the spirit of wisdom.*

(South) *I call upon the warm and quickening light,
For thou art fire and inspiration
Which warms the hearth and heart.*

(West) *I call upon the cool waters of sea and stream.
The realm of our watery beginnings
Tempers our emotions with love and compassion.*

(North) *I call upon flowering field and forest,*
For thou art lands of beauty and pleasure.
Bring forth abundance and great bounty.

(LF) The Lead Female will now consecrate the elements and cast the circle.

(LM) The Lead Male will now call upon the Guardians of the four quadrants.

(C) The Celebrant tones the bell three times, places incense upon the coals, and steps back.

(LM) The Lead Male picks up the bundle of corn on the altar, holds it in offering, and says the following:

Our Lady teaches that naught receives naught,
That as we have sowed, so shall we reap.
On this night all shall receive accordingly.
Nothing shall be withheld from those deserving,
For blessed are the fruits of our labors.

(LM) The Lead Male now hands the corn to the Lead Female (LF). She will hold it in offering as she *invokes the Goddess.* (All participants hold their corn in offering as well).

(All)

Ayea, ayea, Cerridwen
Ayea, ayea, Cerridwen
Ayea, ayea, Cerridwen
Ayea, ayea, ayea.

(LF) The Lead Female now hands the corn back to the Lead Male (LM). He will hold it in offering and *invoke the God.* (All participants hold their corn in offering as well).

(All)

Ayea, ayea, Cernunnos
Ayea, ayea, Cernunnos

Ayea, Ayea, Cernunnos
Ayea, ayea, ayea.

(LM) The Lead Male addresses the group as follows:

Once again has the goddess provided,
For our seeds, once planted, became flowers
And those flowers became the fruit of our desires.
Bountiful is our harvest and great shall be our reward.
We rejoice, as we once again come full cycle.

(All)

Ayea, ayea, Cerridwen
Ayea, ayea, Cerridwen
Ayea, ayea, Cerridwen
Ayea, ayea, ayea.

Ayea, ayea, Cernunnos
Ayea, ayea, Cernunnos
Ayea, ayea, Cernunnos
Ayea, ayea, ayea.

(LF) The Lead Female picks up the John Barleycorn, holds it in offering, and asks the blessing upon it as follows:

Corn and barley are of this Earth,
With love and work we gave them birth.
Though they were just once small seeds,
Through them we achieved our wishes and needs.
Behold john barleycorn, who was our plight,
Now brings us joy and abundance this night,
Because of him we know and see
The truth of our own reality.

(LF) The Lead Female now hands the John Barleycorn to the Lead Male (LM), who will offer him at each quadrant as the Celebrant (C) follows along. When the Celebrant stops at each quadrant, she or he reads the legend of John Barleycorn[2] as follows:

(East) *There were three kings into the East,*
Three kings both great and high,
And they hath swore a solemn oath
John Barleycorn should die.

They took a plough and plough'd him down
Put clods upon his head,
And they hath sworn a solemn oath
John Barleycorn was dead.

But the cheerful spring came kindly one,
And show'rs began to fall;
John Barleycorn got up again,
And sore surpris'd them all.

(South) *The sultry suns of summer came,*
And he grew thick and strong,
His head weel arm'd wi' pointed spears,
That no one should him wrong.

The sober autumn enter'd mild,
When he grew wan and pale;
His bending joints and drooping head
Show'd he began to fail.
His color sicken'd more and more,
He faded into age;
And then his enemies began
To show their deadly rage.

---

[2] This version of "John Barleycorn" is from the book *Egyptian Myth and Legend* by Donald A. Mackenzie.

They've ta'en a weapon long and sharp,
And cut him by the knee;
They ty'd him fast upon a cart,
Like a rogue of forgerie.

(West) *They laid him down upon his back,*
And cudgell'd him full score;
They hung him up before the storm,
And turn'd him o'er and o'er.

They filled up a darksome pit
With water to the brim,
They heaved in John Barleycorn
There let him sink or swim.

They laid him out upon the floor,
To work him farther woe;
And still as signs of life appear'd,
They tossed him to and fro.

(North) *They wasted o'er a scorching flame,*
The marrow of his bones;
But the miller used him worst of all,
For he crush'd him between two stones.

And they hae ta'en his very heart's blood,
And drank it round and round;
And still the more and more they drank,
Their joy did more abound.

John Barleycorn was a hero bold
Of noble enterprise;
For if you do but taste his blood,
T'will make your courage rise.

(LM) The Lead Male now returns to the altar and hands the John Barleycorn to the Lead Female (LF). She holds it in offering and says:

> *Our Lord and Lady shall provide*
> *Long after all has withered and died,*
> *Though they have given us life through the land,*
> *What we now hold is the work of our hand.*
> *And always remember, just as the corn*
> *We like they, are ever dying and reborn.*

(All)

> *As the corn, we are reborn.*

(LF) The Lead Female now breaks off a piece of the John Barleycorn and eats it, she passes it to the Lead Male (LM), who does the same thing. It is then is passed among the members. As the John Barleycorn is passed, each member says *as the corn, we are reborn.*

(C) The Celebrant comes forward, tones the bell three times, and offers his/her corn in thanksgiving for what has been received. As this is a personal time, the thanks need not be said aloud. When the Celebrant (C) is finished, the corn is laid on the floor by the altar. All participants, one at a time, will then come forward and do the same. When everyone has offered their corn, they will take hands and chant the following, raising the energy and directing it into the corn.

> *Corn and grain*
> *Bring joy and gain.*

(LM) and (LF) The Lead Male and the Lead Female will now do the Rite of Union. All will partake in Perfect Love and Perfect Trust.

(C) The Celebrant will now come forward, tone the bell three times, and extinguish the quadrant candles in a widdershins manner (counter-clockwise) as follows:

(North) *Flowering field and forest, land of glorious beauty, may abundance and great bounty be with each of us this night.*

(West) *Cool waters of sea and stream, realm of our watery beginnings, may we always temper our emotions with love and compassion.*

(South) *Warm and quicking light, fire of inspiration, bringer of strength and power, may we always remain steadfast in your ways.*

(East) *Soft and whispering winds, intellect and perception are yours. We ask the spirit of wisdom be with all from this time forward.*

(LM) The Lead Male will now dismiss the Guardians of the four quadrants in a widdershins manner.

(LF) The Lead Female will circumambulate three times widdershins around the circle. Members will follow, holding their corn as they chant:

As the corn, we are reborn.

(LF) The Lead Female will now banish the circle. All members leave, taking their corn with them.

The Rite is ended.

Note: Extra corn may be placed in the circle. This corn can then be cooked after the ritual and added to the feast table.

Autumn Equinox / Mabon

The Autumn Equinox, also known as Mabon, is celebrated sometime around the 21st of September. Again, as with the Spring Equinox, we have a time of equal day and equal night. However, after this night the days grow shorter and the sun begins to wane in power.

This festival is also known as the Harvest Home and is basically the end of the agricultural year. Now all the crops have been gathered. Canning and storage for the winter is a priority, and wine making is in full progress. Some things that come to mind are leaves turning color, bird migrations, corn harvesting, and bonfires.

The purpose of the Autumn Equinox is two-fold. First we want to thank the God and Goddess for all we have *received* and second we want to project for *the ability to maintain* that which we possess. It does no good to manifest a goal if you cannot keep it. This is what the corn baba repre- sents: thanksgiving for what you have received and asking for the ability to keep what you have cre- ated. When constructing your corn baba, bear in mind what you have re- ceived and what you need to maintain. If you were working for a job promo- tion you should have it by now, so you will want to decorate the corn baba with

something which represents your new position. This can be done through the use of color, stones, symbols, or through a simple letter stating your objective, which can be attached to the baba.

Making a Corn Baba

Strip off dried husks from the corn cob and soak them in water until pliable. Use the cob as the body. Use paper, cotton or a small Styrofoam ball for the head. Cover with strips of husks and attach to cob. To create the arms, cut a narrow strip of husk and roll into 7" length. Tie this off at the ends with string. Attach the arms to the cob and then fashion the dress from strips of corn husks, as shown in the drawing. Use the corn silk or yellow yarn for hair. You may add a hat, basket or other things which represent your objective. There should be a larger version of the corn baba for the altar.

A Ceremony for Autumn Equinox

In preparation for this ritual, cover the altar with a brown cloth and place two orange altar candles upon it. You will want the chalice, athame, pentacle, incense burner, bell, and the salt and water bowls. In the center of the altar, a place is left for the corn baba. The pentacle will be in front of her with an orange votive candle upon it. You will need candles for the quadrants in the appropriate colors, a dry red wine and a dry white wine, charcoal, and incense. Baskets of leaves, corn, and dried flowers should be placed at each quadrant. These can be added to the feast table later.

All of the participants will want to bring their corn babas with them into the circle. These will be energized and then taken home and tacked over (or placed near) the main door. Four members are chosen to read the quadrant parts at the appropriate time.

Autumn Equinox / Mabon Ritual
(C) The Celebrant enters the circle; all participants follow with their corn babas. (LM) and (LF) The Lead Male and Lead Female will enter later.

(C) The Celebrant tones the bell three times and then lights the altar candles saying:

> (While lighting the right candle)
> *Lord of the Dark Realm descend,*
> *your strength and power now lend.*

> (While lighting the left candle)
> *Lady of the Moon's Bright Light,*
> *In your name we gather this night.*

(C) The Celebrant tones the bell three times and the (LM) Lead Male and (LF) Lead Female enter with the corn baba for the altar. As they enter they circumambulate three times and all members chant the following:

(All)

> *Blessed are the corn and grain,*
> *For they have brought joy and gain.*

(LM) and (LF) The Lead Male and Lead Female place the corn baba in the middle of the altar.

The four members chosen to read the quadrant parts will now take their places.

(C) The Celebrant will light the quadrant candles and the chosen members will say the following accordingly:

> (East) *Equal day and equal night,*
> *Golden leaves, icy wind, and the dying Sun,*
> *Shadows cast from the fading light,*
> *And the spirit of the harvest is upon us.*

> (South) *Flaming Autumn fires,*
> *The memory of a summer past,*
> *Fills our hearts with warmth and passion,*
> *As we revel in the bounty of the harvest.*

(West) *Water cooled by a setting Sun*
Reflecting the last glimmer of day,
Thou art the twilight, the time of passing.
Now do we realize the wisdom of the harvest.

(North) *Barren land reveals the pitted soil,*
Gathered crops provide food and joy,
Death awaits rebirth,
And the promise of the harvest sustains.

(LF) The Lead Female will now consecrate the elements and cast the circle.

(LM) The Lead Male will now call upon the Guardians of the four quadrants.

(C) The Celebrant will now light the candle in front of the corn baba on the altar saying:

Golden-haired Corn Mother,
Red Dying King,
Leaves turn, sickles gleam
Summer's end is at hand.
Our harvest has been hearty
And our dreams fulfilled.
Blessed is the Autumn fire
Which brings hope and promise;
Blessed be our Lord and Lady
Who brought us life and light.

(All)

Blessed be our Lord and Lady.

(LF) The Lead Female will now do the *invocation of the Goddess.*

(All)

Ayea, ayea, Cerridwen
Ayea, ayea, Cerridwen

Ayea, ayea, Cerridwen
Ayea, ayea, ayea.

(LM) The Lead Male will now do the *invocation to the God*.

(All)

Ayea, ayea, Cernunnos
Ayea, ayea, Cernunnos
Ayea, ayea, Cernunnos
Ayea, ayea, ayea.

(C) The Celebrant will now address the group saying:

This is the time of equal day and equal night,
The time of gathering and celebration,
A time when the abundance of life flows freely,
And yet the chill of death lingers near.
For now the Corn Maiden,
our Silver Moon Goddess,
Offers up her bounty and withdraws,
The Corn King, Red Lion of the South,
giver of life, bringer of death,
Remains ever steadfast.
Now is the time for petitions,
Now is the time for reward,
Now is the time for thanksgiving.

Blessed be the Lady,
Blessed be the corn,
Blessed be the Lord,
Blessed be the harvest.

(All)

Blessed be the Lady,
Blessed be the corn,
Blessed be the Lord,
Blessed be the harvest.

(C) The Celebrant tones the bell three times. Each member will bring his/her corn baba to the altar, hold it in offering, and give thanks for what they have received. The babas are then placed around the altar. All take hands and chant the following to raise the energy to be directed into the babas:

Blessed be the harvest.

(LM) and (LF) The Lead Male and the Lead Female will now do the Rite of Union. All will partake of the wine in Perfect Love and Perfect Trust.

(C) The Celebrant will tone the bell three times and then extinguish the quadrant candles as follows:

(North) *Death is upon us and rebirth will follow, gathered crops provide us with hope and joy, and the promise of the harvest sustains.*

(West) *Twilight and the time of passing is upon us, cool waters reflect the last glimmer of light, bringing us closer to the wisdom of harvest.*

(South) *Our hearts are filled with warmth and passion, autumn fires bring memories of summers past, as we revel in the bounty of the harvest.*

(East) *Shadows cast from golden leaves; the dimming light, the icy wind, and the dying sun—all are part of the spirit of the harvest.*

(LM) The Lead Male will now dismiss the Guardians of the four quadrants in a widdershins (counter-clockwise) manner.

(LF) The Lead Female will now banish the circle in a widdershins manner. All members, carrying their corn babas, will follow her out chanting:

Blessed be the harvest.

The Rite is ended.

The Chapel at Our Lady of Enchantment in preparation for Samhain. The altar of offering in the foreground is decorated with three symbols of the season: the skull for death, the cauldron for transition, and the antler or horn for life.

Samhain / All Hallows Eve

Samhain, which means "Summers End," is cele-brated on October 31st. It is the end of the agricultural sea-son and the beginning of the Celtic New Year. Samhain is the festival of the dead and was Christianized as All Soul's or All Saint's Day. This is a time of chaos and a reversal of normal order; endings and beginnings are occurring si-multaneously.

For our ancestors, Samhain was when the majority of the herd was butchered, providing food for the winter months. Slaughter, barren earth, and decreasing daylight made the concept of death an ever-present reality. Be-cause of this, Samhain has always been considered a time when the veil between the worlds was thin, a night of magic charms and divination, when the dead could be easily contacted.

On this night, through spiritual myth, we see the Goddess of vegetation and growth return to the under-world. For now is the time of the Horned God of the hunt, the God of death and regeneration. It is He who will rule over the winter months, the time of transition when we switch from life to death. Just as Beltane was a time of life and growth, Samhain is its opposite: a time of death and decay.

On an individual basis, this is the time to rest and re-evaluate our lives and goals. Now is when we want to get rid of any negativity or opposition which may surround our achievements or hinder future progress. Samhain should have seen the accomplishment of our desires, and so now we need to stabilize and protect what we have gained. This is important, because it is impossible to con-centrate—let alone put energy into new goals—if what we have is not secure. Therefore we will want to bind off all interference with what we are doing so we can begin something new at Yule.

For this ceremony, you will want to make a protection talisman. I suggest you write out your needs (what you wish to protect) on a piece of parchment paper. Place this paper into a small bag with other objects, herbs and stones which represent your request. These things 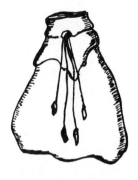 should all have some naturally inherent protective qualities about them. Each circle member's bag will be placed in the center of the circle and charged during the ritual. You then keep it until Beltane, at which time it is burned or buried with the knowledge it has accomplished its purpose.

A Ceremony for Samhain

In preparation for this ritual, cover your altar with a black cloth and place two black altar candles upon it. There should be a cauldron with a red candle in it to represent the dying light and the promise of the light's return. Skulls, bones, and animal skins are good decorations at this time, as they bring the death aspect into perspective. The athame, incense burner, chalice, dark red wine and dry white wine are also needed, along with the pentacle, an extra black candle, charcoal, spicy seasonal incense, the bell, and four carved pumpkins with candles in them. The four pumpkins are placed at each quadrant. A small basket will be needed in which to put all of the member's talismans. These talismans will be charged with energy during the ritual.

Samhain/All Hallows Eve Ritual

(LM) The Lead Male will announce the beginning of the ceremony, light a black candle, and lead the group into the ritual area. All will circumambulate three times as they chant the following:

(All)

> Death brings life,
> Life brings death.

(C) The Celebrant will tone the bell three times and then light the altar candles, saying the following:

> (While lighting the right candle) Blessed be our Lord of Death,
> For he brings rest and regeneration.

> (While lighting the left candle) Blessed be the Death Crone,
> For she transforms the soul of man.

(C) The Celebrant tones the bell three times.
(LF) The Lead Female will enter with the lighted cauldron and circumambulate three times as all chant the following:

(All)

> Death brings life,
> Life brings death.

(LF) The Lead Female stops and faces (LM) the Lead Male, who will then welcome her as follows:

(LM) Maiden of Darkness
Mother of the Moon,
Crone of Death
What treasure dost thou bestow
Upon your lord?

(LF) My Lord I bring thee the secret
of life, which death shall not deceive.

She then hands (LM) the Lead Male the cauldron.

(LM) Bless thee Death Crone,
Lady of transformation,
For I shall be as one in service,
Thy protector and guide.

(C) The Celebrant tones the bell three times and proceeds to light the four quadrants as follows:

(East) *Let there be light in the East,*
The home of the Eternal Spirit.

(South) *Let there be light in the South,*
The home of the Divine Spark.

(West) *Let there be light in the West,*
The home of the rest and Regeneration.

(North) *Let there be light in the North,*
The home of the Final Atonement.

(LF) The Lead Female will now consecrate the elements and cast the circle.

(LM) The Lead Male will now call upon the Guardians of the four quadrants, holding the cauldron in offering as he does so at each.

(C) The Celebrant tones the bell three times.

(LM) The Lead Male hands the cauldron to the (LF) Lead Female, who will now do the *invocation to the Goddess*.

(All)

Ayea, ayea, Cerridwen
Ayea, ayea, Cerridwen
Ayea, ayea, Cerridwen
Ayea, ayea, ayea.

(LM) The Lead Male addresses the group as follows:

We gather together this night
In a place that is not a place,
And a time which is not a time.
All that was green has died,
And memories are our retribution and reward.
For now the season of life draws to a close,
So begin the dark times of rest and re-evaluation.

(LM) and (LF) The Lead Male and Lead Female now take hands and face the altar, saying the following:

(LM) Blessed is the Death Crone,
And her silent tides of death and birth,
For she alone brought love,
Life and wisdom to our Earth.

(LF) Blessed is the Dying King,
And the sacrifice of blood he shed,
For he alone will guide us
Through the time of darkness and dread.

(All)

Ayea, ayea, Cerridwen
Ayea, Ayea, Cerridwen

Ayea, Ayea, Cerridwen
Ayea, ayea, ayea.

Ayea, ayea, Cernunnos
Ayea, ayea, Cernunnos
Ayea, ayea, Cernunnos
Ayea, ayea, ayea.

(C) The Celebrant tones the bell three times and then takes the basket to each member who will in turn place his or her talisman in it. The Celebrant returns to the altar and hands the basket to the Lead Male (LM) saying:

All honor to our Horned God, Cernunnos,
Lord of Death, Guardian of Mysteries
Prince of Darkness.
Bless now these tokens of our esteem,
And let it be so that that which is not in accord
With thy ways shall henceforth be banished.

(All)

All honor to thee Cernunnos,
Lord of Death, Guardian of Mysteries,
Prince of Darkness.

(LM) The Lead Male holds the basket in offering and will now do the *invocation to the God.*

(All)

Ayea, ayea, Cernunnos
Ayea, ayea, Cernunnos
Ayea, ayea, Cernunnos
Ayea, ayea, ayea.

(C) Holding the basket, the Celebrant faces the group and says the following:

As with life, so with death,
We have come full circle.
Let us now bid farewell to all
Which has not been productive.
The past does not bring sadness,
But produces guidance for the future.
All which passes away shall make room
For what we wish to bring about.

(C) The Celebrant places the basket in the center of the circle and instructs all members to take hands and chant the following to energize the talismans:

As life recedes,
Death fills our needs.

(LM) and (LF) The Lead Male and Lead Female will now do the Rite of Union to bless the wine for all to partake of in Perfect Love and Perfect Trust.

(LF) The Lead Female faces the group and says the following:

Let us bid farewell to our Lady fair and dear,
And pray she will return to all of us next year.
Let us welcome back our Lord powerful and bright,
As he shall be our protection from winter's plight.
All hail, Cerridwen and Cernunnos.

(All)

Ayea, ayea, Cerridwen
Ayea, ayea, Cerridwen
Ayea, ayea, Cerridwen
Ayea, ayea, ayea.

Ayea, ayea, Cernunnos
Ayea, ayea, Cernunnos

Ayea, ayea, Cernunnos
Ayea, ayea, ayea.

(C) The Celebrant tones the bell three times and then extinguishes the quadrant candles as follows:

(North) *Death now brings darkness to the North,*
The home of the Final Atonement.

(West) *Death now brings darkness to the West,*
The home of Rest and Regeneration.

(South) *Death now brings darkness to the South,*
The home of the Divine Spark.

(East) *Death now brings darkness to the East,*
The home of the Eternal Spirit.

(LM) The Lead Male will now dismiss the Guardians of the four quadrants in a widdershins (counter-clockwise) manner, beginning with the North.

(C) The Celebrant will now extinguish the altar candles, until the area is left in total darkness except for the lighted cauldron:

(While extinguishing the left candle)
Blessed be the Death Crone,
For she transforms the soul of man.

(While extinguishing the right candle)
Blessed be the Lord of Death,
For he brings rest and regeneration.

(LF) The Lead Female will now banish the circle in a widdershins manner beginning in the North.

The candle in the cauldron is allowed to burn out completely. All members will take their talismans with them.

The Rite is ended.

This now completes the Eight Great Sabbats rituals. Through these rituals, we express our desires as well as our appreciation to the God and Goddess. These ceremonies are not carved in granite and can be changed to fit the size and structure of the group working with them. However, it is imperative that you keep them within the framework for which they were designed. By this I mean, when it is time to plant you plant; and when it is time to receive you do likewise. In this way you are working with the flow of the universe and building power and energy, which will project your desire in the proper manner.

A good thing to remember when working with times of power (or any magical situation) is "only ask for what you need and you will ever abound." Magic is a tool, and when properly used will benefit all concerned. However, only the practitioner can control what will manifest as the end result.

—— CHAPTER TEN ——

The Art of Spellcasting

Talismans, Amulets and Candle Magic

In this chapter, we are going to explore the basic precepts of spellcasting. The primary focus is on the use of candles, talismans, amulets, and various symbolic objects. This chapter also contains the actual formulas for individual spells.

Like any other form of magic, spells always work best when they are properly performed, under controlled conditions. They also allow you another form of expression and and an occasion to work toward your desires. By taking advantage of the extra time between full moons and Sabbats, you are able to reinforce and reaffirm your goals.

Just what is a spell and how is it different from a ritual? A spell is a *period of time* during which an object, person or situation is held in a captive state for the benefit of the person working his or her will and intent. This is accomplished by selecting and using words, music or chants that have a dominating effect over the recipient. Spells result in direct and dynamic effects and usually get immediate results. On the other hand, a ritual is a prescribed event

175

or ceremony, built up by tradition and repetition. Rituals must be repeated several times to be effective, whereas most spells need only be done once in order to achieve results.

Unfortunately, there is a disadvantage to simple spellcasting that isn't present with ritual work. The drawback is in the quality and durability of the results. Spells act fast and are easily and quickly done, but the results are not as long lasting as those of a formal ritual. However, there are those moments when something is needed in a hurry and there just isn't time for a formal ritual. This is what spells were made for, immediate action and help with a problem.

Out of all magic, spellcasting is the most popular, the easiest, and the most convenient with which to work. Spells do not require any specific amount of room and can be done almost anywhere with a minimal amount of equipment. However, as with all magic, the art of spellcasting has its guidelines and rules. These are necessary for achieving effective results. The three major factors to consider before starting a spell are:

- Necessity
- Proper ingredients
- Focused energy

Necessity: What is it that you want, better yet, really need? How emotionally involved are you with your present desire or goal? Without the proper emotion and the total involvement of focused energy, the spell will not work. You don't just sit around casting spells for lack of anything else to do. Also, you—and only you—are totally responsible for what you do or don't do. It is not up to others to judge your secret desires, but it is up to you to attempt to fulfill them. You, and only you, can make yourself happy. No one else can do it for you. Other people can't make you happy, they just momentarily distract you from some desire or inner conflict.

Proper ingredients: This is where so many make the biggest mistake, not using the exact ingredients called for in a spell. Don't substitute. If you don't have the *exact* items you need, wait until you are able to get them. You can fool the ego, but not your higher self—and this is where your power comes from. Don't take short cuts. If the spell calls for marigolds, it doesn't mean basil. If the burning time for a candle is two hours, then it must burn for two hours, not one hour and ten minutes because you have other things to do.

Focused energy: This is the personal power that you project because of an emotional tie with the objective. The need, desire, and total lustful involvement must be there or the energy level will not be high enough to cause a reaction. One hundred percent of your attention must be given at the moment of action; you must force your intent out and into the atmosphere. It is your personal power and energy which makes a spell work. You can have all the right ingredients, but if the energy or enthusiasm is not there, then this will be reflected in the results or lack thereof.

Spells, like rituals, require a certain amount of planning and preparation. If you are creating the spell yourself, then you will need to plan your spell so it will coincide with the proper phase of the moon or planetary energy. The spell will also have to be arranged in a logical manner so as to accomplish what it is you wish in the least amount of time. And, you should make a check list, as you do with a ritual, of all the items you will need or be using. Here are some helpful hints and important points to remember when preparing for spell-working:

Spellcasting Tips

- Assemble all of the ingredients that will be used.

- Label each package of herbs, incense, and all oils with their contents and purpose.

- Put all of the items you will need together in a box or in a bag.

- If you are going to do a spell several times, be sure to plan it so that you are able to repeat it at the same time every day.

- Be sure to read over the spell several times so that you know exactly what you will be doing.

- *Never, never eat before ritual or working magic*. You should cut out all meat, milk products, and heavy foods at least twelve hours prior to any magical operation. It is also good to restrain from sexual activity for this period as well. Food tends to ground us, and sexual activity will dissipate and subdue vital energy.

The Talisman

The word talisman means to "consecrate." It is exactly this process of "consecration" which converts the object you are using into an effective *active* magical channel for working your will. This consecration process can be part of a spell or ritual, or it can be done separately. In most cases, the spell or ritual itself will serve to consecrate the talisman.

MacGregor Mathers[1] defined a talisman as "a magical figure charged with the force it is intended to repre-

---

[1] MacGregor Mathers was a ceremonial magician and author of related books, as well as a founder of the Golden Dawn.

sent." A talisman should be constructed to attain a definite result. It is not like an amulet which is generally used for bringing good luck or warding off evil. An efficient talisman should be capable of operating in such a way that its effectiveness is obvious immediately, or at least within seven days of its construction.

> **Talismans are actively charged objects constructed to attain a definite result.**

Talismans can be made to do all sorts of things: to acquire money, obtain patronage, recover lost property, influence people, obtain knowledge, disrupt friendships, compel someone to love you, and protect your property and loved ones.

The thing to remember about talismans is that once created and charged, they can be left to do their work—without further attention. This is because the energy set up by the operator continues to work over a set period of time. Talismans work like a battery and have the benefit of being self-recharging to some extent (if their construction has been carried out correctly). This recharging ability is due to the relationship between the talisman and its corresponding symbolic force.

The Amulet

The amulet is an object that has been left in its virgin state and is then psychically charged or energized with a specific purpose in mind. Amulets are usually used for protection, as they are passive in their communicative abilities. Only when their barriers have been crossed do they react or retaliate. A good example would be the horseshoe over the door which brings luck to all who cross beneath it; or the protection amulet that wards off the negativity of others when they come in contact with it.

Almost any symbolic object can be turned into an amulet. Special stones, shells with markings, wood carvings, statues—anything which already exists or is in a natural state can be turned into an amulet simply by forcing your will and dynamic energy into it. Because of the amulet's passive nature and the fact that most of its power resides in its intrinsic symbology, there is no need to formally consecrate it.

> **Amulets are passive; their power resides in their natural symbology.**

Candles and Magic

Candles are automatically magical because they bring light to the darkness. They are illumination, and represent the vitalizing power of the sun. Candles are a symbol of light and the individual soul. Just as the flame consumes the wax, so candles illustrate the relationship between spirit and matter.

Candles can be used by themselves as a form of magic, or they may be incorporated as part of a spell. In either case, the candle itself becomes the point of focus. The color of the candle, its shape and size all play an important role in the art of candle magic. The color signifies the intent; design or shape represents the objective; and the size is equivalent to the amount of time needed for burning.

Burning time frames (or how long the candles should burn) are among the most important aspects of candle magic. Each color of the spectrum has its own special wave length or vibrational frequency. Therefore, the amount of time you will need to burn the candle you are working with must be considered before beginning (or writing) a candle magic spell. The following chart gives both the color significance as well as burning time frames for the candles.

Color Magic Correspondances

Color of Candle	Meaning of Color	Burning Time
Red	Courage, strength, survival, power, lust, immediate action.	One hour
Pink	Love, friendship, opening the heart, calming the emotions.	One hour
Orange	Action, attraction, selling, bringing about desired results.	Two hours
Yellow	Communication, selling oneself, persuasion, attraction.	Three hours
Green	Love, fertility, money, luck, health, personal goals.	Four hours

Blue	Creativity, tranquillity, peace, perception, patience.	Three hours
Dark blue	Wisdom, self-awareness, psychic abilities, the ability to cause changes.	Two hours
Purple	Power, ambition, tension spiritual development, power over others.	One hour
Black	Protection, returning or releasing negativity, power, create discord.	One hour
Brown	Stability, grounding, earth rites, to create indecision.	Four hours
Gold	Prosperity, attraction, wealth, for attracting money, increase.	One hour
White	Universal color; can be used for any work. Use frame for altar candles or all general candle magic.	No set time

In addition to their differences in color, candles also come in a variety of shapes other than the simple household taper. There are image candles in the shape of men and women, animal shapes such as the cat, candles which have been notched or made into knobs, and even candles that are shaped like skulls. It is a good idea to use the symbolic candles whenever possible. Because they are already formed into an image of your desire, they makes the visualization process of your spell all that much easier.

The first step is to choose a candle by selecting a color or shape which represents your desire. Next you will have to *dress* the candle. This is done by anointing the entire candle with a special oil. The oil is usually made of some plant or flower that also represents your desire. Place some of the oil on your fingertips. As you concentrate on your desire, rub the oil onto the candle, starting from the center and rubbing upward. Then rub the oil from the center downward, (as pictured). Be sure to cover the entire candle with the oil.

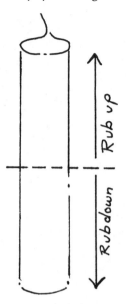

When you are planning a candle magic spell try to keep all keep all of your symbolism or vibrations the same. For example, if you were doing a love spell you would want to use a red image candle and love-drawing oil. If you were trying to open up the lines of communication between you and another person, you might want to try a yellow candle and Mercury oil. For a peaceful home, use a blue candle, tranquillity oil, and maybe some sandalwood incense. The whole idea is to keep your colors, objects, and thoughts similar in meaning and symbology. By doing this, your energy is focused for maximum effect. When special oils are not available, you can always use a good quality olive oil.

Symbolic Objects

All magic hinges upon the relationship between emotion and expressed energy. Symbols create automatic responses to people, places, and situations. It is this sudden response, coupled with directed emotion, that creates the desired outcome. The wonderful thing about most magic, especially spellcasting, is almost any ordinary object can serve as the response trigger.

For instance, take dolls. How many times have you picked up a doll or stuffed toy and remarked on how it looked like someone you knew? A photograph of a loved one creates an instant emotional response. The painting in the museum triggers a past life; the statue in the garden speaks to you. These may be ordinary objects to others but they bring out special feelings and emotions to you. This is what magic is all about, bringing emotions to the surface so their energy can be focused and directed towards a desired outcome.

A picture or figure of a dragon can be turned into a protective amulet and placed near the door. The broom, once activated and charged, can be used to clear negative vibrations and energies from the room. Small pillows shaped like hearts and filled with special herbs can be made into love amulets and placed where a loved one will sit. Almost any box or bag can be turned into a talisman by adding some special stones, a picture, some herbs, and magical sigils. In fact, your entire house could be one giant magical talisman, from the front door to the back. No one would know for sure what you were doing. However, your close friends would surely notice the feeling of peace and tranquillity they had whenever they came to visit.

Remember, magic is the practical way to reach your goals. It is not to be abused, nor is it to be feared. It is just another process of getting what you want. The spells in the following chapter were designed for this very purpose. They will help to influence the forces and your surroundings so that things go in your favor.

CHAPTER ELEVEN

A Practical Magic Formulary

Spells for All Occasions

The following spells are ones which I have been teaching people for years. They are simple to perform and don't require impossible-to-find ingredients. In fact, most of the items used in these spells are readily available in your own home or can be purchased through any occult mail order house. For those who are so inclined, the recipes for some of the oils and incenses are included in the Appendix II.

Be sure to read through the spell you will be doing several times. Don't forget to make your ritual check list and organize all items needed prior to the work. And last but not least, you are the best judge of what you need and are able to maintain. If you doubt what you are doing or feel bad about it, then you have no business doing it. On the other hand, if it feels right and you are willing to accept responsibility for your actions, then GO FOR IT.

The spells presented here are divided into four categories: love, prosperity, protection, and miscellaneous. Each spell is complete, listing the ingredients, the proper timing, and exact step-by-step instructions for its performance. Remember, properly executed spells work. So don't make substitutions or try to take short cuts and you will be successful.

Spells to Attract Love

The Love Box

Items needed: A small heart shaped box, love-drawing incense, love-drawing oil, a pink candle, parchment paper, pen, rose quartz, some of your own hair, orris root powder, charcoal, and matches.

Perform this spell on the first Friday after the Moon turns New. To prepare, center and ground yourself. Light the charcoal. Inscribe upon the parchment that which you specifically desire in a lover. Place some love-drawing incense upon the coals. Dress the pink candle with love-drawing oil, while saying:

> *May the Gods of Love hear my plea,*
> *And bring everlasting love to me !*

Light the candle and read your petition aloud, then place the candle on top of the parchment paper. Place more incense upon the coals. Meditate upon your wish, and when finished, read the following:

> *Hail to thee Goddess of Love,*
> *Shine down on me from above.*
> *Bring now a lover to me*
> *As I will so it shall be.*

Let all items remain until the candle has burned out. Fill the love box with the following items: one pinch of incense, seven drops of oil, parchment paper, rose quartz, some candle drippings, your hair, and some orris root powder. The box is now left where it will be most effective.

A Spell To Attract a Desirable Lover

Items needed: one large spice jar, painted pink and decorated with red ribbon and lace; one red candle; your birth stone; one teaspoon basil, the love drawing sigil. (Figure 1)

The night before the Full of the Moon, take all of the items and go to a secluded spot. Light the red candle. As the wax drips, add the basil to it a little at a time. When the candle has been totally consumed and all of the basil has been added, shape the warm wax into a heart saying:

> *Wax to heart—thou art transformed,*
> *Two become one—and love be warmed.*

Before the wax cools completely, place the birth stone in the center of the wax heart. Put the wax heart with the embedded stone into the jar. Place the jar on top of the sigil. The jar should now be consecrated with salt, water, incense, and fire. Then hold the jar in your power hand, and place it against your heart, saying:

Fig. 1

Elements and powers that be,
Let love now come unto me.
By the heart and by the stone,
I'll no longer be alone.
Come to me, come to me.
As I will, so it shall be.

Keep this jar in the bedroom. Whenever you go on a date or out to a club, take the heart with you or place it in the room where you plan to entertain a special guest.

Candle of Love Spell

Items needed: Picture of the desired one, and some of their hair and handwriting to use as relics. You will also need a red cloth pouch, one red image candle, rose petals, and rose oil.

Place the candle in front of you with the picture and all of the needed items in front of it. Dress the candle with the rose oil as you picture your lover coming closer to you and being more attentive. When you feel the time is right, light the candle and chant the following to build power and energy. Direct this energy into the candle:

Candle of power,
From this hour,
Bring unto me
The love that I see.
That he shall requite
My attentions this night,
Let him see only me.
As I will, so mote it be.

Allow the candle to burn completely out. Carry the pouch filled with the rose petals and your lover's items with you whenever you are going to be together. It is also a good idea to wear some of the rose oil.

Love Binding Spell

Items needed: Two red dolls filled with foxgloves, clove, orris root, blessed thistle, coriander, yarrow, and Solomon seal; tag lock[1] of the couple to be bound, a 21-inch red cord. love-drawing oil, love-drawing incense and burner, red candle and holder, charcoal and matches.

Begin on the Monday closest to the New Moon and perform for seven consecutive days, ending on a Sunday. Prepare to do this work by centering and grounding yourself. Light the charcoal. On a small table, place the red candle in the center. Carve both of your names on the candle. Place some love-drawing incense on the coals. Dress the candle with love-drawing oil as you chant the following:

> *Candle of Love,*
> *Work me this spell,*
> *That the one I do love*
> *Shall love me as well.*

Light the candle and place more incense on the coals. Take each doll and pass it first through the incense, then quickly through the candle flame, saying the following:

> *Air and Fire,*
> *Bring forth my desire.*

---

[1] Tag locks and relics are items which have belonged to the individual you are working on—items such as handwriting, hair, finger nail clippings, clothing, blood.

Place each doll seven inches apart from the candle and then chant the following seven times:

> *I enchant you by Earth and Heaven*
> *Turn to me, turn to me, turn to me*
> *By seven.*
> *Through moonlight and black of night,*
> *All my love you shall requite.*
> *Think of me and think of pleasure,*
> *Turn to me in daily measure.*
> *Turn to me, turn to me, turn to me.*
> *As I will, so mote it be.*

Repeat this spell for the next six days. Each time, move the dolls one-inch closer to the candle. On the last day, the dolls should touch the candle. Then let the candle burn completely out. Bind the dolls together with the red cord and secret them away to a special place where both of you are sure to meet.

Talisman to Attract Love

Items needed: One green silk pouch, the Second Pentacle of Venus (Figure 2), one green candle, Venus incense and Venus oil, matches and charcoal, 1/2 teaspoon basil, needle and green embroidery thread, a square of green construction paper, and a pen.

Fig. 2

Perform this spell on a Friday during the Waxing Moon, during the hour of Venus. Take the green pouch and sew the symbol for Venus

(♀) on both the front and back, using the green thread. Using the green paper, make two Venus Pentacles. Place the basil in the middle of these with the pentacles facing outward. Glue them together.

Dress the green candle with the Venus oil, light some of the Venus incense, and as you pass the Venus Pentacle through the candle flame and the incense smoke, chant the following seven times :

> *Pentacle of Air, Pentacle of Fire*
> *Filled now with my desire,*
> *Bring me love, bring me passion*
> *As this talisman I now fashion.*

Put the pentacle in the bag. Place the bag next to the green candle. When the candle has completely burned out, put the talisman in your purse or pocket and carry it with you.

Note: Love spells work well to get someone's attention or to give a relationship a chance, *but it is unwise to use them to try to hold someone against their will.* When this is done, the only thing keeping the person with you is the energy of the spell. *The first time you forget or aren't able to do the spell, then the energy is gone and the relationship is over.*

Prosperity Spells

Attraction / Personal Success

Items needed: Yellow altar cloth, success incense, yellow candle, attraction oil, First Pentacle of the Sun (Figure 3), charcoal and matches.

Time: This spell should be done on a Sunday morning during the Waxing of the Moon.

Light the charcoal and place some success incense upon the hot coal. In your mind's eye, see yourself being successful in all you do. Take the yellow candle and dress it with the attraction oil. As you do this, see clearly what you want coming to you. As you are rubbing the oil on the candle, chant the following:

> *Power of the Rising Sun,*
> *Let success to me now come.*

Light the candle and place some more incense upon the coals. Now take the Sun Pentacle and pass it through the candle flame and the incense smoke as you say the following six times:

> *This talisman shall bring to me*
> *Honor, wealth and prosperity.*

Place the talisman beneath the candle and chant the following, forcing all your energy into the candle and the talisman:

> *Success and prosperity*
> *come to me,*
> *As I will, so mote it be.*

Allow the candle to burn for one hour. Repeat this ritual for six days. On the sixth day allow the candle to burn out and carry the Sun Pentacle with you at all times.

Fig. 3

Personal Success Pouch

Items needed: Medium-sized gold pouch, success oil, success incense, gold candle, gold parchment paper, marigolds, cedar wood, Herkimer diamond, charcoal, and matches.

The best time to perform this spell is the first Sunday after the New Moon at 12:00 noon. This spell should be performed six times.

Center and ground yourself. Light the charcoal. Write on the parchment your desired goal. Place some success incense upon the coals. Take the pouch and add to it a pinch of marigold and cedar, then put the Herkimer diamond in the pouch. Dress the candle with success oil, while visualizing yourself manifesting your desired goal and reaping its rewards. Light the candle and chant the following:

> *Mighty Ones of Wealth and Power*
> *Let my goal manifest from this hour!*

Place some more incense on the coals. Read the parchment with your desired goal upon it aloud, then read the following:

> *Powers of Nature, Sun, Earth and Tree*
> *Lend me your strength, as I call upon thee*
> *Bring personal success, and my desired goal to me.*
> *And as I will, so mote it be !*

Repeat this spell for a total of six New Moons. On the last day, take the pouch and fill it with the following: Six drops of success oil, a pinch of success incense, the parchment paper, candle stub, and the rest of the marigolds and cedar. That same day, take the pouch and bury it at the foot of an oak tree. Never return to it, lest you break the spell.

Jupiter Prosperity Talisman

Items Needed: Jupiter Pentacle (Figure 4), Jupiter incense, jasmine herb, an orange candle, a small bottle of olive oil, a pin with which to write on the candle, charcoal and matches.

Three days before the Full Moon, take the packet of herbs and put them into a bottle of olive oil. Use a small bottle and keep it sealed tightly. On the night of the Full Moon, find some place where you can be alone. On a small table, place all of the items needed. When all is ready, take several deep breaths, relax and clear your mind. You are then ready to begin. Light the incense as you say:

> *Let the Spirit of Air grant me insight*
> *And wisdom to accomplish my desire.*

Relax, take a couple more deep breaths, and begin to visualize what it is you want or are trying to accomplish. Pick up the candle and carve your name on one side and your desire on the other. Now, as you visualize what it is you want, pour a small amount of the oil in your hand and rub this all over the candle, while you chant the following:

> *Success and prosperity*
> *come to me*
> *As I will, so mote it be!*

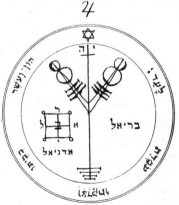

Place the candle in the candle holder and light it. Again, visualize what it is that you want. Pick up the Jupiter Pentacle, hold it in both hands, and chant the following (while raising as much energy as you can):

Fig. 4

This talisman shall bring to me
Honor, wealth and prosperity
As I will so mote it be!

Place the talisman under the candle. Allow the candle to burn for two hours. Repeat this spell for three days. Each time you perform the spell, rub the oil on the candle and allow it to burn for two hours. On the last day, let the candle burn out and then carry the Talisman with you in your purse or pocket. This is good for getting a job, a raise in pay, for good luck in gambling, and otherwise acquiring money.

First Pentacle of the Sun *(For Prosperity)*

The First Pentacle of the Sun from the Key of Solomon transmits the countenance of the Almighty, at whose aspect all creatures obey and to whom the Angelic spirits do reverence on bended knees. The face on the pentacle is that of the great Angel Methraton.

Items needed: A replica of the First Pentacle of the Sun (Figure 5), a small gold pouch in which to carry it, and some marigold seeds.

On the first Sunday after the New Moon, take your pentacle and marigold seeds and go into the woods or a garden. Stand so that you are in the direct rays of the sun. Hold up the pentacle and the seeds so that the rays of the sun shine directly on them and charge them both by chanting the following:

Fig. 5

> *Almighty One of Wealth and Power,*
> *Thou shalt be at my side from this hour.*
> *Bring me wealth and with blessings shower*
> *Let my prosperity from this time flower.*

Now plant the seeds as you visualize each flower representing your personal gain and increase in prosperity. Keep the pentacle with you at all times, and at least six times a day recite the chant. This should be done until your flowers are in bloom. You will then take one of the flowers and place it in your bag with the pentacle. Dry the others for further use.

Spell to Attract Money

Items needed: A green candle, five silver coins, a small jar filled with sea water, your magic wand, and some matches.

On the night of the full moon, go into the woods to a spot where four paths cross. Here you will inscribe with your wand a large circle with a pentagram in the center. Dig a small hole in the very center and place the jar in it so the top half is exposed to the moonlight. Place the green candle on top of the jar. Light it as you chant the following:

> *My Lady of the Abundant Sea,*
> *Bring me wealth and prosperity.*

Now take the silver coins and place one on each point of the pentagram as you chant the following:

> *Silver coins that sparkle bright,*
> *Increase my wealth five-fold this night.*

When the candle is completely burned out, open the jar. Pick up each of the silver coins one at a time, and place them into the jar as you chant the following;

> *Earth to Sea, Earth to Sea,*
> *Bring me the money I now see.*
> *As I will, so mote it be!*

Sprinkle a drop or two of the water on the ground and thank the Goddess for her blessings. Bring the water home with you and anoint yourself with it every day until it is gone.

Protection Spells

Pentacle Protection Spell

Items needed: A pentacle pendant, protection oil, protection incense, a white candle, salt and water, charcoal, and matches.

This spell is best performed on the night of the Full Moon. Three days prior to the Full Moon, place the pentacle in the salt bowl. Completely cover it with the salt to cleanse and purify it. Center and ground yourself. Light the charcoal. Dress the candle with protection oil while chanting:

> *May the Gods give blessings to me this night*
> *And protect me now within your light.*

Add some protection incense to the coals and light the candle. Remove the pentacle from the salt bowl and pass it through the incense smoke and the flame of the candle. Sprinkle it with water and say:

By Earth, protect my world
By Air, protect my mind
By Fire, protect my desire
By Water, the forces I bind.
O Pentacle of Power, protect me from this hour.
May the Spirit of the Holy Light
Protect me ever more this night !

Stay there and leave everything as it was until the candle burns out completely. Then put all items away and wear the charged pentacle at all times.

Saturn Protection Spell *(Reversing Negativity)*

This spell is to help protect as well as return all negative thoughts and vibrations which are sent your way.

Items needed: One black candle, one mirror, two Saturn Pentacles (Figure 6)—one large one to place upon the back of the mirror, and one to carry with you at all times.

Glue the Saturn Pentacle to one side of the double-sided mirror. Then make another smaller Saturn Pentacle that you can carry with you at all times. This should be drawn in black ink on white parchment paper. Take the mirror and place it so the reflective side faces the direction from which the negativity is coming. Take the black candle and hold it firmly in your right hand as you focus your attention. When you feel ready, chant the following:

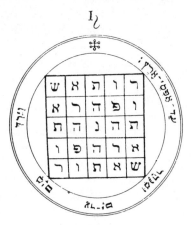

Fig. 6

Candle black, Saturn's power
Reflect back from this hour
Negative thoughts sent to me
As I will, so mote it be

Now light the candle. Put it on top of the small pentacle and allow it to burn for one hour. Repeat this procedure for three consecutive nights. On the last night, allow the candle to burn out. Carry the small pentacle with you at all times.

The Mirror Box

Items needed: One cigar box, black construction paper, a black cat candle, Saturn oil, Saturn incense, a thurible (incense burner), a picture of the one who brings you harm, strong glue, scissors, charcoal, matches, and an assortment of mirrors. (Plastic mirrors are great because they can be cut with an X-acto® knife.)

Glue the construction paper to the outside of the cigar box, and let dry before continuing. The next step is to glue the mirrors to the inside of the box, with the shiny part facing inward. This means that when you open the box, you will see the shiny mirror side facing you, mirroring your reflection. Gluing the mirrors may take some time to complete, but the box will last you many years. Let the box dry completely for a few days before you begin the spell.

The mirror box is a tool used to repel negative thoughts and vibrations. The mirrors will act as a shield, bouncing all energy back to the sender with the power of the Three-Fold Law. This is a tool for protection; you are only repelling the energy which was sent to you back to its source.

Begin on a Thursday night, just before the Moon turns New. Set up a small table facing the direction where your enemy lives. Put the mirror box on the table. Set the candle on top of the box. place the picture so that it faces you and leans up against the candle. Light the charcoal. Set the thurible (incense burner) in the front of the box, together with the Saturn oil.

Dress the cat candle with Saturn oil. This will absorb and burn away all negativity that surrounds you. Light the candle. Place some Saturn incense upon the coals, and say:

> *Saturn is my power and from this hour*
> *All negativity sent to me is reflected back and returned to thee.*
> *This magical box shall hold and contain you,*
> *And all your negativity shall now turn against you.*
> *I send back all hatred by the law of three.*
> *And as I will, so mote it be !*

Place some more incense on the coals. Open the box and place the picture inside. Close the lid and let the candle burn for one hour on top of the box.

Repeat this spell for three consecutive nights. On the third night, (which should be on Saturday since you began this spell on a Thursday) put the candle stub inside the box, along with the picture, and leave for at least one lunar cycle. This spell may be repeated monthly. Always keep the box closed when you are not doing the spell. After the negativity has been cleared, take the picture and candle stub and bury it away from your home.

Goddess Protection Spell

Items needed: Salt and water, power oil, white candle, white parchment paper, silver-blue pouch, charcoal, protection incense, a medium-sized clear quartz crystal.

Add nine pinches of salt to the water while saying:

> *Salt and water, now combine*
> *Protect my heart, protect my mind.*
> *Dark evil forces now fade away*
> *So that only good shall come my way.*

Sprinkle mixture around the area in which you are working. Inscribe the protection symbol (Figure 7) on the parchment paper. Dress the candle with power oil and then place it on the parchment paper. Place some incense on the coals. Pick up the crystal and hold it over the flame as you say the following:

> *Goddess of the Moon I call upon thee*
> *For your love and blessings.*
> *Great Mistress of all magic, protect me*
> *And give me your power in this my hour of need.*

Take some power oil and rub it on your lower abdomen. Take some time to meditate and reflect on the work done. Place the parchment, the vial of oil, and the crystal into the pouch and carry it with you. When you feel negative energies coming at you, rub the oil on your solar plexus and hold the crystal in your power hand.

Fig. 7

Miscellaneous Spells

Spirit Guide Channeling

This simple exercise will enable you to contact your Spirit Guide and/or help to get messages or information from the cosmos.

Items needed: One white skull candle, angelic vibrations incense, spirit oil, a pillow or meditation mat, a dish or incense burner filled with white sand, and charcoal.

Arrange a special space for the skull candle. It should be either a shelf or a pedestal, high enough so that when you are sitting on your meditation mat or pillow, you have to look up to see the candle. Place the dish for incense between the mat and the candle.

Be sure you will not be disturbed. Turn down the lights. Stand behind the mat (or pillow) and take several deep, relaxing breaths to get yourself into the mood to contact higher forces.

Take the candle and dress it with the spirit oil, charging life into the candle. Make the candle a receptacle for the spirit (or universal consciousness) which will soon inhabit it. Then place it on the shelf or pedestal. Take several deep breaths and feel the atmosphere in the room change to become a chamber of spirituality. Now light the candle, saying the following:

> *O Lord of Life, Goddess of Delight*
> *Open my mind, let my soul take flight*
> *That now your knowledge shall come through*
> *As my thoughts and essence become one with you.*
> *So shall it be!*

Sit down on the mat or pillow. Take several more deep breaths; relax. Place some incense on the coals and begin to merge with the candle. Visualize the energy of the cosmos form a swirling cone of white light above the skull. See this energy funnel down into the skull, giving it life and a personality of its own. Then draw this energy from the skull in a stream of light, making a connection between you and the skull. It is through this connection that the information you are seeking will travel. Relax and allow yourself to accept the information which is being transmitted. Record all information which has been received by keeping a journal. When all has been completed, snuff out the candle and put all items away.

Peaceful Home Spell

This spell is especially useful for those who entertain on a business level. There are times when people of varying viewpoints may need to come together in a social atmosphere. To keep things running smoothly, harmoniously, and peacefully, use this spell prior to the party.

Items needed: One blue candle, tranquillity oil, sandalwood incense.

One hour before the party, take your ritual bath. As you are doing this, visualize the guests as they arrive. See in your mind's eye the evening progressing and everyone having a wonderful time. When your bath is completed, anoint your solar plexus with the tranquillity oil. This will help you project a positive and harmonious energy level throughout the evening.

Take the blue candle and place it in the room where most of the evening's activities will be held. Now take the incense, light it, and carry it throughout the house. Move from room to room saying:

> *Queen of Heaven, Star of the Sea,*
> *Fill this house with love and harmony*

Silver goddess enthroned above
Let all gather here in peace and love.
So be it.

Now enter the room where you have placed the blue candle and light it. Walk around that room four times in a deosil (clockwise) fashion chanting, just as you did with the other rooms. Place the incense next to the candle and wait for your guests.

Spell for Peace and Harmony

Items needed: Rose quartz, mirror, one pink candle.
Light the pink candle and place it in front of the mirror. Hold the rose quartz in your hands and gaze at the flame reflected in the mirror as you chant the following:

O Blessed and reflected light
Bring to me peace this night,
Let my mind and heart be free
And filled with love and harmony.

Look past the flame into the mirror. Try to see what negative elements are affecting you that you want to get rid of. See them being drawn from you into the candle flame and then into the mirror. When you feel the time is right, place the mirror face down. Allow the candle to burn for one hour and then snuff it out. Clean the mirror in salt water and repeat whenever needed.

The Invocations and Rites of Union

The Invocation to the Goddess

This invocation is used at both Sabbat and Full Moon ceremonies, where it calls for the "Invocation to the Goddess." This is always done by a woman,[1] as the intention is to draw the essence of the Goddess down into the practitioner, thereby intensifying the feminine energy within the circle. If there is no woman available, it is common practice for one of the male participants to read the invocation rather than to actually do it. Please note that the God and Goddess names of Cernunnos and Cerridwen have been used. These my be changed to suit the needs and pantheons of different traditions. The important factor is the

---

[1] During group ceremonies, the invocation to the Goddess is always done by a female participant, just as the invocation to the God would be done by a male participant. However, during a private ritual, there is no reason why a man could not do the invocation to the Goddess or a woman the invocation to the God.

transference of energy during the invocation. Therefore, it is essential to work or call upon only those forces with which you are most familiar.

The Invocation

Thou who whispers gentle yet strong
Thou for whom my soul doth long,
By most men you are seldom seen
Yet you ever reign as Virgin, Mother, Queen.
Through the veil you pass with pride
As I beckon thee now to be at my side,
                              Cerridwen.

Thou who knows, thou who conceals
Thou who gives birth, thou who feels,
For you are the Goddess and Mother to all
Pray thee now come as I call,
Now through the mist, I hear your voice
And invoke thee most gracious Goddess by choice,
                              Cerridwen.

Thou who suffers as all men die
Doth with her victim in love lie,
For you are the Goddess and Crone of despair
To our ending we all must share,
I feel thy passion and feel thy presence
I desire to be one with thy vital essence,
                              Cerridwen.

I pray thee dancer of eternal bliss
Bestow upon me thy wondrous kiss,
Let now thy light, love and power
Descend, become one with me this hour.

For you are the Creatress of Heaven and Earth
To my soul and spirit you have given birth,
                    Cerridwen.

The Invocation to the God

The invocation of the God, like that of the Goddess, is used during most Sabbat ceremonies or any ritual where the male God force is desired. It is, of course, performed by the male leading the group—or if there are none present, it could be read aloud by one of the female members.

The Invocation

Father of Death, Father of Night
Father of Birth, Father of Light
        Cernunnos, Cernunnos, Cernunnos.

Come by flame, come by fire
Come now, whom we desire
        Cernunnos, Cernunnos, Cernunnos.

O' Horned One, O' Ancient One
God of the Sun, Bringer of Light
The Powers of Darkness put to flight.

O' Horned One, O' Ancient One
Who comes from beyond the gates of Death and
Birth
Come who gives life to all on Earth,

Come I invoke thee
For you are Pan, Apollo, Cernunnos,
Lord of Hades, Lord of Death
You are them all, yet you are He
Come, come my lord as I beckon thee.

Come, come my Lord of wild delights
Come, join with us in these secret-mystic rites
Come, come my Lord of fire and flame
As I call out your sacred and holy name
    Cernunnos, Cernunnos, Cernunnos.

Invocation to Oshun

Oshun is one of the most beloved deities (Orishas) of the Yoruba pantheon. She is one of the Seven African Powers in the practice of Santeria and considered by most to be a Goddess of love, beauty and civilization. She has also been known to bestow wealth upon those she favors. Her day is Saturday, her color is yellow or gold, and her number is 5. The pumpkin is sacred to her, as are mirrors, honey, bells, and the fan.

The following invocation to Oshun is aimed at bringing both love and beauty to whoever calls upon her.

The Invocation

My Lady of Charity, I now beckon thee
To descend, come down, be one with me.
Oshun I revere you, love you above all
Hear me my Lady, and come as I call,
    Oshun, Oshun, Oshun.

Goddess of rivers, life bringer to Earth
Enter my soul, to my dreams give birth.
As I am the child, so you are the Mother
Before you there shall stand no other,
        Oshun, Oshun, Oshun.

Our union prevails from centuries past
Binding and bonding our hearts at last.
Whenever I call, whenever I need
You shall be there, you shall give heed,
        Oshun, Oshun, Oshun.

As I now honor thee, and follow your ways
Guide me and guard me throughout all my days,
Let now your Spirit become one with me
As this is my desire, so now it shall be,
        Oshun, Oshun, Oshun.

The Blessing of the Cakes and Wine

The Blessing of the Cakes and Wine is a sacrament. The purpose of this ceremony is to sanctify the specially prepared cakes and wine. When everyone partakes of the cakes and wine, they are blessed and encouraged by the higher spiritual forces of the God and Goddess.

The Blessing of the Cakes and Wine is usually performed by the male (LM) and female (LF) leaders of the ritual in which it is taking place. Red wine or its non-alcoholic equivalent is placed in the chalice prior to the ritual and covered with a white cloth. The cakes are placed on a small plate or upon the pentacle and covered with a white cloth.

The (LM) and (LF) stand in front of the altar, then genuflect or bow. (LM) will pick up the cakes and (LF) will pick up the chalice filled with wine. The cakes and wine are then held in offering to the God and Goddess as (LM) and (LF) recite their lines respectively:

(LF) *She who appears with the first dawning and*
Is clouded in the mists.
Her hair is pearled with dew as she emerges
From the Sea of Life.
Her beauty blinds the eye, her fragrance stirs
The heart like a distant song.
For veiled is the blessed virgin to whom the
Waters are the strength of life.
Reborn from darkness is she who brings forth
Hope renewed.
Let now the blessings of the great Moon Mother de-
scend,
Become one, and unite within this sacred vessel.

(LM) *I have felt his touch, the warmth of his light*
And the power which comes from the new dawning
day.
His potential is strength, his presence is passion
and
His seed brings forth new beginnings.
For holy art thou, lord of the universe,
Formed in beauty and strength
Thou art our single source of light and life
Without which we would not be.
Let now the blessings of the Great Sun Father de-
scend,
Become one, and unite within this sacred meal.

The Lead Female (LF) and the Lead Male (LM) will now each exchange wine and cakes with each other, as they do so they each will say "Perfect Love and Perfect Trust." The cakes and then the wine are passed amongst the other participants in "Perfect Love and Perfect Trust." The leftover wine and cake is left upon the altar for those who wish to come in after the ritual has ended and pay their own special respects, again partaking of the blessed wine and cakes.

The Rite of Union

The Rite of Union is almost a ritual unto itself. For it is during this rite that the red and white wine actually become the vital essence of the God and Goddess. Once this process has been completed, the sacred fluid is poured into the chalice (the physical symbolic representation of the Goddess) and conjoined with the athame (the physical symbolic representation of the God) to form the perfect union of masculine and feminine energy.

Our traditional seasonal rites come to us from ancient fertility cults. Although we do not place the high importance in physical fertility, in procreation, that our ancestors did, the idea is still valid. Because fertility has always been associated with good fortune and abundance, it seems only natural to incorporate this concept into rituals designed to celebrate the life cycles.

For the Rite of Union you will need two containers of wine. One is filled with white wine and the other with red wine. The chalice and athame (or ritual dagger) are also needed.

The Rite of Union is performed by the male and female leaders of the group. They approach the altar, then genuflect or bow. He (LM) will pick up the chalice and she

(LF) will pick up the containers of wine. They then turn and face each other. She holds the wine as pictured and he will kneel facing her, holding the chalice as pictured.

(LF) The Lead Female now pours the red and white wine into the chalice, combining them as she says the following:

> *I pour the red and the white, that they shall mix*
> *As life and death, joy and sorrow, peace and humility,*
> *And impart their essence and wisdom unto all.*

(LM) The Lead Male remains kneeling as he holds the chalice filled with wine saying:

For I am the Father, Lover and Brother unto all,
The bringer of life, the giver of death,
Before whom all time is ashamed.
Let my spirit breathe upon you
And awaken the fires of inspiration
Within your soul.

(LF) The Lead Female places the containers of wine on the altar, then picks up the athame or dagger. She slowly lowers it into the chalice as the Lead Male (LM) rises with the chalice to meet the blade of the athame so it touches the wine within. While doing this, they will speak as follows:

(LF) *For as this athame represents the male and the God,*
(LM) *So this chalice represents the female and the Goddess.*

(LM & LF) *And they are conjoined, to become one, in truth, power and wisdom. So mote it be.*

(LF) The Lead Female places the athame (dagger) upon the altar. (LM) The Lead Male takes a sip of the wine, hands it to (LF) saying "Perfect Love and Perfect Trust." (LF) takes a sip and passes it back to the (LM) saying the same. The chalice is now passed to each member of the group in Perfect Love and Perfect Trust.

The Solitary Rite of Union

This is a simplified version of the actual Rite of Union and is used on those occasions where the individual wishes to draw upon the energy of the of the God and

Goddess for personal reasons when working in a solitary capacity.

> *My Lord is the power and the force of all life*
> *My Lady is the vessel through which all life flows,*
> *My Lord is life and death*
> *My Lady is birth and renewal,*
> *The Sun brings forth life*
> *The Moon holds it in darkness.*

At this point plunge the athame into the chalice as you continue with the following:

> *For as the Lance is to the male,*
> *So the Grail is to the female*
> *And together they are conjoined to become one*
> *In Truth, Power and Wisdom.*

At this point, offer the chalice to the God and Goddess and then drink, absorbing the energy of this vital essence.

Correspondences, Recipes and Magical Lore

A Solitary Full Moon Ritual

Items needed: Two white altar candles, a chalice, the athame, a pentacle, incense burner, incense, charcoal, quadrant markers, and a bell. You will also need the salt and water bowls (filled with salt and water), and whatever object, candle, or talisman is being charged.

The Ritual

Perform this ritual the night of the Full Moon. Enter the circle area, circumambulate three times deosil (clockwise) and then bow or genuflect before the altar. Light the altar candles while saying the following:

> (While lighting the right candle)
> *Holy art thou, Lord of the Universe,*
> *For you are my power and might.*

(While lighting the left candle)
Holy art thou, Lady of all Creation,
For you are my life and light.

Light the quadrant candles, consecrate the elements and cast the circle as instructed in Chapter Seven. Tone the bell six times and do the *invocation to the Goddess*. If you are using a working candle, light it now. Hold the candle (or whatever you are wishing to energize) in offering to the moon Goddess as you say the following:

My lovely Lady Cerridwen
The time of magic draws near.
I beseech thee my Lady, hear
My invoking words and appear.
For as I stand within your light
Be with me and bless my magic this night.

Personal petitions are now offered. Tone the bell nine times and then do the Solitary Rite of Union to bless the wine. Tone the bell six times and say the closing prayer:

Blessed be my Lady
Mother unto all,
Thou who was before all mankind
You are my hope and inspiration,
For you have been with me from the beginning
And you shall be with me at the end of time,
I ask your blessings this night,
Be with me now and forever.
So mote it be.

Tone the bell three times, banish the circle, and extinguish the altar and quadrant candles.

Elemental Correspondences

East

Direction:	East.
Archangel:	Raphael.
Qualities:	Light, intellect, new beginnings.
Color:	Blue.
Meaning:	To know.
Zodiac:	Gemini, Aquarius, Libra.
Tattvic symbol:	Circle.
Season:	Spring.
Magical Tool:	Wand or dagger.
Animal:	Eagle.
Symbols:	Sky, wind, clouds, incense.
Elemental Spirit:	Sylphs.
Elemental King:	Paralda.
Positive Characteristics:	Intelligence, mind, psychic abilities.
Negative Characteristics:	Lack of communication, gossip, memory problems.

South

Direction:	South.
Archangel:	Michael.
Qualities:	Activity, force, willpower.
Color:	Red.
Meaning:	To will.
Zodiac:	Aries, Leo, Sagittarius.
Tattvic Symbol:	Triangle.
Season:	Summer.
Magical Tool:	Dagger or wand.

South (continued)

Animal:	Lion.
Symbols:	Fire, sun, passion and candles.
Elemental Spirit:	Salamanders.
Elemental King:	Djyn.
Positive Characteristics:	Energy, enthusiasm, will, strength.
Negative Characteristics:	Greed, vengeance, ego, jealousy.

West

Direction:	West.
Archangel:	Gabriel.
Qualities:	Heavy, passive, receptivity.
Color:	Green.
Meaning:	To dare.
Zodiac:	Cancer, Scorpio, Pisces.
Tattvic Symbol:	Crescent Moon.
Season:	Fall.
Magical Tool:	Chalice.
Animal:	Snake, Scorpion.
Symbols:	Waves, bodies of water, cups.
Elemental Spirit:	Undines.
Elemental King:	Niksa.
Positive Characteristics:	Sensitivity, compassion, grace.
Negative Characteristics:	Overly emotional, insecurities, lack of self-esteem.

North

Direction:	North.
Archangel:	Auriel (Uriel).
Qualities:	Stability, growth, manifestation.
Color:	Yellow.
Meaning:	To keep silent.
Zodiac:	Taurus, Virgo, Capricorn.
Tattvic Symbol:	Square.
Season:	Winter.
Magical Tool:	Pentacle.
Animal:	Bull.
Symbols:	Mountains, forest, stone, salt.
Elemental Spirit:	Gnomes and trolls.
Elemental King:	Gob.
Positive Characteristics:	Endurance, reliability, material world.
Negative Characteristics:	Materialistic, non-progressive and lazy.

Herbs of the Zodiac

Aries (THE RAM): Fire, Cardinal: Allspice, cactus, dragon's blood, pepper.

Taurus (THE BULL): Earth, Fixed: Alfalfa, honeysuckle, primrose, tulip.

Gemini (THE TWINS): Air, Mutable: Almond, clover, lavender, pine.

Cancer (THE CRAB): Water, Cardinal: Lemon balm, cucumber, lilac, thyme.

Leo (THE LION): Fire, Fixed: Basil, coriander, hyssop,tobacco.

Virgo (THE VIRGIN): Earth, Mutable: Corn, magnolia, vetivert, wheat.

Libra (THE SCALES): Air, Cardinal: Broom, eyebright, lily of the valley, mint.

Scorpio (THE SCORPION): Water, Fixed: Belladonna, hemlock, lotus, willow.

Sagittarius (THE ARCHER): Fire, Mutable: Asafoetida, garlic, rosemary, wormwood.

Capricorn (THE GOAT): Earth, Cardinal: Cypress, patchouli, mugwort, vervain.

Aquarius (THE WATER BEARER): Air, Fixed: Benzoin, linden, mistletoe, papyrus.

Pisces (THE FISHES): Water, Mutable: Crocus, heather, myrrh, yarrow.

Incense and Oils

Love-Drawing Incense

Combine the ingredients and put them into a small glass container or spice jar. This incense can be used in all love-drawing rituals.

1/4 cup red incense base[1]
1 teaspoon basil
2 tablespoons rose buds
1/2 teaspoon rose oil

Love-Drawing Oil

Combine the following oils in a small bottle. Add a small piece of rose quartz and one small rose bud. During the waxing of the moon, place the bottle where the moon can shine upon it.

1 part rose oil
1 part musk oil
1 drop cherry oil

Success Incense

On the first Sunday morning after the New Moon, mix the following ingredients together and place them in a small plastic bag within a yellow or gold pouch.

1/4 cup gold incense base
2 tablespoons marigolds
2 tablespoons myrrh
1 teaspoon ambergris oil
1/2 teaspoon myrrh oil

Success Oil

Mix the ingredients together and pour into a dark bottle. Place the bottle in direct sunlight for one hour.

1 part ambergris oil
1 part myrrh oil

---

[1] Incense base is a colored powder made of dried paint and sawdust or talcum powder. It can be purchased at an occult store or ordered through a catalog.

Success Oil *(continued)*

> 1 part storax oil
> 1 pinch marigolds
> 1 pinch gold glitter

High Altar Incense

For use in all rituals. During the Waxing Moon, mix the following ingredients together and place them in a special container. Keep this container on your altar.

> 1/4 cup brown incense base
> 1/4 cup frankincense
> 1/4 cup sandalwood
> 1/4 cup myrrh
> 1 teaspoon frankincense oil
> 1 teaspoon myrrh oil
> 1 clear quartz crystal (place the crystal in the container).

High Altar Oil

In a special dark bottle, again during the Waxing of the Moon, mix the following oils together. Place a small, clear quartz crystal in the bottle.

> 1 part frankincense oil
> 1 part myrrh oil
> 1 part sandalwood oil

Protection Incense

During the Waning Moon, mix the ingredients together to form the incense. Place the incense in a black box. Put a piece of black onyx in the box. Place a black candle on top of the box and light it. Allow the candle to burn out. The incense is then ready to use.

>1/4 cup black incense base
>1/4 cup patchouli leaves
>2 tablespoons dragon's blood resin
>2 tablespoons copal
>2 tablespoons patchouli oil
>2 tablespoons frankincense oil
>2 drops camphor oil

Protection Oil

During the Waning of the Moon, mix the following oils together in a small black bottle, along with a piece of broken mirror, a wad of black thread, and a straight pin.

>1 part patchouli oil
>2 parts frankincense oil
>1 part camphor oil
>2 parts sandalwood oil
>1 part rosemary oil

Recipe for John Barley Corn

Preheat oven to 375° F
In a bowl, mix together the following:

>1-1/2 cubes of butter
>1/2 cup honey
>1-1/2 cups rolled oats
>1 cup mixed grains (barley, wheat, etc.)
>1 cup coconut and sesame seeds (mixed)
>2 teaspoons salt

Take the mixture out of the bowl and put it on a cookie sheet. Form the mixture into the shape of an anatomically correct male figure.

Bake at 375° F for one-half hour. It is a good idea to make this the day before Lughnasadh so that it is ready for the ceremony. Once John Barley Corn has been baked and cooled, place him on a suitable tray and cover with a white cloth.

A Cycle, A Season, A Turning of the Wheel

Past, present and future become one when we enter the bounds of the magic circle. The wheel turns, and time stands still. Shadows dance while the flickering candlelight evokes images from deep inside in our souls. Protected by the God, embraced by the Goddess, long forgotten myths and legends speak to the child within. Although they are only simple stories, they explain the cycles of life, the seasons of change, and bring us hope for the future.

The Myth of Esus and Tarvos Trigaranus

Long ago when the world was young, a marvelous and wonderful thing happened. In the early spring, near the well of Coventina,[1] a beautiful bull-calf was born. At first glance you could see that it was not an ordinary bull[2]. His coat was golden-red and his form was perfect. His eyes were clear and bright and intelligent.

The bull was no sooner up and about, running and playing, when out of the sky descended three stately cranes[3]. They danced about him in a circle, delighted with his beauty and energy. The bull was happy too. He liked his new friends who could sing and dance and fly. He was respectful of them, too, and bowed his head, for he knew they had come from the Great Sky Father.

As spring wore on into early summer, the bull grew exceedingly fast and was soon fully grown. Never was there a bull like this one. His fame spread far and wide. Animals, men and Gods came to look upon his great beauty. The cranes were his constant companions and because of this the bull became known as Tarvos Trigaranus (bull with three cranes).

Their days were filled with endless enjoyment. The world was bright and beautiful and full of flowers. For in the ancient times, the world had never known the winter.

Now, there was a hunter God named Esus (lord-master). He roamed through fields and forests looking for an animal worthy of his passion, but he found none to be of satisfaction.

Early one beautiful morning, he happened upon the meadow where Tarvos and the three cranes were sleeping. One glance at the bull and Esus new his search had ended. He drew his blade and came upon the sleeping

---

[1] Coventina is the triple-aspected, patron Goddess of the sacred well at Carrawburgh, Northumberland, in Britain.

[2] The bull has always been a primal symbol of strength and potency, representing the fertilizing and generative power of nature.

[3] Cranes symbolize language and thought. They represent love and a zest for life. They are considered a symbol of spring.

bull, but the cranes saw the danger and gave out the cry of alarm.

The bull rose to do battle with Esus. The bull's horns were formidable weapons. The God Esus and the divine bull Tarvos clashed in combat. They fought all day and all night but neither could seem to beat the other. The contest continued in this manner for days.

Then, on the night of the Dark of the Moon, the bull began to fail in strength. And there, under the great oak tree, Esus struck Tarvos, the divine bull, a deadly blow. His blood poured out upon the roots of the tree and its leaves turned golden-red at that very instant for pure shame and grief. The cranes made a great crying sound. One of them flew forward and in a small dish caught up some of the bull's blood. Then the cranes departed, flying toward the south.

A gloom descended upon the world. The flowers wilted and the trees dropped their leaves. The great sun withdrew its warmth. The world grew dark and cold and snow fell for the first time. Every man and beast prayed to the Great Earth Mother to bring back the warmth, or all would soon perish. She heard, and took pity on all of nature. Soon the light began to return.

The three cranes came flying back from the south, and one still had the dish. It flew to the great oak tree where Tarvos, the divine bull, had been slain. The crane then poured the blood upon the ground. Suddenly out of the dust sprang a bull-calf, reborn from the Great Earth Mother.

All nature rejoiced. The warmth of the sun returned. Grass and flowers sprang up. The leaves budded out on the trees. Spring came again to the world.

In time the hunter-god, Esus, heard of the bull's rebirth and sought to find him. This was the beginning of the cycle which even to this day persists. Esus, the hunter god, ever overcomes the divine bull, but our Great Mother Earth ever causes him to be reborn.

And so it is with all of nature. Spring brings forth life, the summer makes it strong, the fall causes it to weaken, and the winter brings its death. We cannot control it or change it, but we can learn to understand and work with it.

—— RECOMMENDED READING ——

There is no such thing as a bad book. A book may be poorly written, and not to your taste, but this does not make it bad. All books contribute in some way to our personal growth, even if the only thing we glean from them is what not to do.

When one enters the field of magic it is always best to consider as many viewpoints as possible before making judgments. I say this because it is difficult to determine what will or will not work, unless you have a thorough understanding of the subject. The following list of selected books offers a variety of opinions and perspectives which will help you to grow and progress in the magical arts.

The suggested reading has been divided into four sections. Section I books are basic and recommended for the individual who is just starting out. Section II books are on an intermediate level and are recommended for those who have some magical training and experience. Section III deals with advanced reading and is intended for the initiate who wishes to expand his or her awareness. Section IV is strictly dedicated to reference books and these are of value to everyone.

Recommended Reading

I. (Basic)
Campanelli, Pauline. *Ancient Ways*. Llewellyn Publications. This book focuses on seasonal celebrations and the practice of magic on a daily basis.

Cunningham, Scott. *Earth Power: Techniques of Natural Magic.* Llewellyn Publications. How to work with the forces and elements of nature. Contains spells and simple magic.

Cunningham, Scott. *Earth, Air, Fire & Water: More Techniques of Natural Magic.* Llewellyn Publications. This book continues where *Earth Power* left off and offers more rites and spells.

Green, Marian. *The Elements of Natural Magic.* Element Books. How to bring magic back into your life and attune to the seasons.

K, Amber. *True Magic: A Beginners Guide.* Llewellyn Publications. This book stresses ethics and magical guidelines.

Valiente, Doreen. *Natural Magic.* Phoenix Publishing. Tap into the magic of flowers, herbs and traditional spells.

Weinstein, Marion. *Positive Magic.* Phoenix Publishing. This is a good introduction to the field of magic.

II. (Intermediate)

Ashcroft-Nowicki, Dolores. *The Ritual Magic Workbook.* The Aquarian Press. A twelve month plan of self-initiation into ceremonial magic.

Bias, Clifford. *Ritual Book of Magic.* Samuel Weiser, Inc. This book has a lot to offer on ritual, the charging of tools, chanting, and magical advice.

Gray, William G. *Western Inner Workings.* Samuel Weiser, Inc. This book provides an overview of the different aspects of Western Magic.

Green, Maran. *Magic for the Aquarian Age*. The Aquarian Press. A contemporary textbook of practical magical techniques.

González-Wippler, Migene. *The Complete Book of Spells, Ceremonies & Magic*. Llewellyn Publications. This book is highly recommended, as it deals with all aspects of magic.

King, Francis & Skinner, Stephen. *Techniques of High Magic*. Destiny Books. This book provides clear and concise information on the tools, instruments and practices of High Magic.

III. *(Advanced)*

Gray, William. *Magical Ritual Methods*. Samuel Weiser, Inc. This book contains the "hows and whys" of ceremonial magic.

Gray, William. *Temple Magic*. Llewellyn Publications. All aspects of the temple on the material plane are examined.

Heisler, Roger. *Path to Power*. Samuel Weiser, Inc. The subject of power is introduced on personal, psychic and universal levels.

Kraig, Donald Michael. *Modern Magic*. Llewellyn Publications. A complete study of modern Western magic done in lesson form.

Regardie, Israel. *Foundations of Practical Magic*. The Aquarian Press. This is an introduction to the Qabalah and includes extensive meditative techniques.

Stewart, R. J. *The Underworld Initiation*. The Aquarian Press. This book is a study of Western symbology and deals with both oral and written tradition. An absolute must for anyone practicing magic.

IV. (Reference)

Bletzer, June G. *Encyclopedic Psychic Dictionary*. The Donning Company.

Cooper, J. C. *An Illustrated Encyclopedia of Traditional Symbols*. Thames and Hudson.

Cooper, J. C. *The Aquarian Dictionary of Festivals*. The Aquarian Press.

Cotterell, Arthur. *A Dictionary of World Mythology*. G. P. Putnam's Sons.

Cunningham, Scott. *The Complete Book of Incense, Oils & Brews*. Llewellyn Publications.

González-Wippler, Migene. *The Complete Book of Amulets & Talismans*. Llewellyn Publications.

Mathers, MacGregor S. L. *The Key of Solomon, the King*. Samuel Weiser, Inc.

STAY IN TOUCH

On the following pages you will find listed, with their current prices, some of the books now available on related subjects. Your book dealer stocks most of these, and will stock new titles in the Llewellyn series as they become available. We urge your patronage.

However, to obtain our full catalog, to keep informed of new titles as they are released and to benefit from informative articles and helpful news, you are invited to write for our bi-monthly news magazine/catalog. A sample copy is free, and it will continue coming to you at no cost as long as you are an active mail customer. Or you may keep it coming for a full year with a donation of just $7.00 in U.S.A. & Canada ($20.00 overseas, first class mail). Many bookstores also have *The Llewellyn New Times* available to their customers. Ask for it.

Stay in touch! In *The Llewellyn New Times'* pages you will find news and reviews of new books, tapes and services, announcements of meetings and seminars, articles helpful to our readers, news of authors, advertising of products and services, special money-making opportunities, and much more.

The Llewellyn New Times
P.O. Box 64383-Dept. 166, St. Paul, MN 55164-0383, U.S.A.

• • •

TO ORDER BOOKS AND TAPES

If your book dealer does not have the books described on the following pages readily available, you may order them direct from the publisher by sending full price in U.S. funds, plus $3.00 for postage and handling for orders *under* $10.00; $4.00 for orders *over* $10.00. There are no postage and handling charges for orders over $50. Postage and handling rates are subjectd to change. UPS Delivery: We ship UPS whenever possible. Delivery guaranteed. Provide your street address as UPS does not deliver to P.O. Boxes. UPS to Canada requires a $50 minimum order. Allow 4–6 weeks for delivery. Orders outside the U.S.A. and Canada: Airmail—add retail price of book; add $5 for each non-book item (tapes, etc.); add $1 per item for surface mail.

FOR GROUP STUDY AND PURCHASE

Because there is a great deal of interest in group discussion and study of the subject matter of this book, we feel that we should encourage the adoption and use of this particular book by such groups by offering a special "quantity" price to group leaders or "agents."

Our Special Quantity Price for a minimum order of five copies of *Reclaiming the Power* is $29.85 cash-with-order. This price includes postage and handling within the United States. Minnesota residents must add 6.5% sales tax. For additional quantities, please order in multiples of five. For Canadian and foreign orders, add postage and handling charges as above. Credit card (VISA, Master Card, American Express) orders are accepted. Charge card orders only may be phoned free ($15.00 minimum order) within the U.S.A. or Canada by dialing 1-800-THE-MOON. Customer service calls dial 1-612-291-1970. Mail Orders to:

LLEWELLYN PUBLICATIONS
P.O. Box 64383-Dept. 166 / St. Paul, MN 55164-0383, U.S.A.

Prices subject to change without notice.

HOW TO MAKE AND USE A MAGIC MIRROR
by Donald Tyson

There's a "boy mechanic" at home in every one of us. As Henry Ford put the world on wheels, Donald Tyson is now opening New Worlds with simple psychic technology.

Author Donald Tyson takes the reader step-by-step through the creation of this powerful mystical tool. You will learn about:

- Tools and supplies needed to create the mirror
- Construction techniques
- How to use the mirror for scrying (divination)
- How to communicate with spirits
- How to use the mirror for astral travel

Tyson also presents a history of mirror lore in magic and literature. For anyone wanting their personal magical tool, *How to Make and Use a Magic Mirror* is a must item.

0-87542-831-2, 176 pgs., mass market, illus.   **$3.95**

EARTH GOD RISING
THE RETURN OF THE MALE MYSTERIES
by Alan Richardson

Today, in an age that is witnessing the return of the Goddess in all ways and on all levels, the idea of one more male deity may appear to be a step backward. But along with looking toward the feminine powers as a cure for our personal and social ills, we must remember to invoke those forgotten and positive aspects of our most ancient God. The Horned God is just, never cruel; firm, but not vindictive. The Horned God loves women as equals. He provides the balance needed in this New Age, and he must be invoked as clearly and as ardently as the Goddess to whom he is twin.

The how-to section of this book shows how to make direct contact with your most ancient potentials, as exemplified by the Goddess and the Horned God. Using the simplest of techniques, available to everyone in any circumstance, *Earth God Rising* shows how we can create our own mystery and bring about real magical transformations without the need for groups, gurus, or elaborate ceremonies.

0-87542-672-7, 256 pgs., 5-1/4 x 8, illus., softcover   **$9.95**

THE BOOK OF GODDESSES & HEROINES
by Patricia Monaghan

The Book of Goddesses & Heroines is an historical landmark, a must for everyone interested in Goddesses and Goddess worship. It is not an effort to trivialize the beliefs of matriarchal cultures. It is not a collection of Goddess descriptions penned by biased male historians throughout the ages. It is the complete, non-biased account of Goddesses of every cultural and geographic area, including African, Japanese, Korean, Persian, Australian, Pacific, Latin American, British, Irish, Scottish, Welsh, Chinese, Greek, Icelandic, Italian, Finnish, German, Scandinavian, Indian, Tibetan, Mesopotamian, North American, Semitic and Slavic Goddesses!

Unlike some of the male historians before her, Patricia Monaghan eliminates as much bias as possible from her Goddess stories. Envisioning herself as a woman who might have revered each of these Goddesses, she has done away with language that referred to the deities in relation to their male counterparts, as well as with culturally relative terms such as "married" or "fertility cult." The beliefs of the cultures and the attributes of the Goddesses have been left intact.

Plus, this book has a new, complete index. If you are more concerned about finding a Goddess of war than you are a Goddess of a given country, this index will lead you to the right page. This is especially useful for anyone seeking to do Goddess rituals. Your work will be twice as efficient and effective with this detailed and easy-to-use book.

0-87542-573-9, 456 pgs., 6 x 9, photos, softcover   **$17.95**

MAGICAL RITES FROM THE CRYSTAL WELL
by Ed Fitch

In nature, and in the earth, we look and find beauty. Within ourselves we find a well from which we may draw truth and knowledge. And when we draw from this well, we rediscover that we are all children of the Earth.

The simple rites in this book are presented to you as a means of finding your own way back to nature; for discovering and experiencing the beauty and the magic of unity with the source. These are the celebrations of the seasons; at the same time they are rites by which we attune ourselves to the flow of the force—the energy of life. These are rites of passage by which we celebrate the major transitions we all experience in life.

Here are the Old Ways, but they are also the Ways for Today.

0-87542-230-6, 160 pgs., 7 x 10, illus., softcover   **$9.95**

ENOCHIAN MAGIC: A Practical Manual
by Gerald J. Schueler
The powerful system of magic introduced in the 16th century by Dr. John Dee, Astrologer Royal to Queen Elizabeth I, and as practiced by Aleister Crowley and the Hermetic Order of the Golden Dawn, is here presented for the first time in a complete, step-by-step form. *There has never before been a hook that has made Enochian Magic this easy!*

In this book you are led carefully along the path from "A brief history of the Enochian Magical System," through "How to Speak Enochian," "How to Invoke," "The Calls," "Egyptian Deities" and "Chief Hazards" to "How to visit the Aethyrs in Spirit Vision (Astral Projection)." Not a step is missed; not a necessary instruction forgotten.
0-87542-710-3, 270 pgs., 5-1/4 x 8, illus., softcover $12.95

THE MAGICAL DIARY
by Donald Michael Kraig
Virtually every teacher of magic, whether it is a book or an individual, will advise you to keep a record of your magical rituals. Unfortunately, most people keep these records in a collection of different sized and different looking books, frequently forgetting to include important data. *The Magical Diary* changes this forever. In this book are pages waiting to be filled in. Each page has headings for all of the important information including date, day, time, astrological information, planetary hour, name of rituals performed, results, comments, and much more. Use some of them or use them all. This book was specially designed to be perfect for all magicians no matter what tradition you are involved in. Everybody who does magic needs *The Magical Diary*.
0-87542-322-1, 240 pgs., 7 x 8-1/2, otabound $9.95

LIFE FORCE
by Leo Ludzia

A secret living energy—as ancient as the Pyramids, as modern as Star Wars. Since the beginning of time, certain people have known that there is this energy—a power that can be used by people for healing, magick, and spiritual development. It's been called many names: Mana, Orgone, Psionic, Prana, Kundalini, Odic force, Chi and others.

Leo Ludzia puts it all together in this amazing new book Life Force. This is the first book which shows the histories and compares the theories and methods of using this marvelous energy. This force is available to us all, if only we know how to tap into it. Ludzia shows you how to make devices which will help you better use and generate this Life Force. This specialized information includes easy-to-follow-directions on: how to build and use pyramids, Orgone Generators such as those used by Wilhelm Reich, and how to make and use the "Black Box"designed and used by the genius inventor T. G. Hieronymus.

Unlike some New Age books, this is a title that will appeal to everyone! Scientists, psychics, occultists and mystics of Eastern and Western paths will want to read this book. It will also attract those people who are interested in psionics, radionics, UFOs and Fortean phenomena.

0-87542-437-6,192 pgs., mass market, illus.   **$3.95**

MODERN MAGICK
by Donald Michael Kraig

Modern Magick is the most comprehensive step-by-step introduction to the art of ceremonial magic ever offered. The eleven lessons in this book will guide you from the easiest of rituals and the construction of your magickal tools through the highest forms of magick: designing your own rituals and doing pathworking. Along the way you will learn the secrets of the Kabbalah in a clear and easy-to-understand manner. You will also discover the true secrets of invocation (channeling) and evocation, and the missing information that will finally make the ancient *grimoires*, such as the **Keys of Solomon**, not only comprehensible, but usable. *Modern Magick* is designed so anyone can use it, and is the perfect guidebook for students and classes. It will also help to round out the knowledge of long-time practitioners of the magickal arts.

0-87542-324-8, 608 pgs., 6 x 9, illus., softcover   **$14.95**

POWER: The Power to Create the Future
by Eric Mitchell
Each of us has something special about us. Each of us has a unique vision, a meaning and purpose to our life, with which we can be the most successful, the most fulfilled, and the most happy. The discovery and fulfillment of that unique vision is your life purpose and will bring with it your highest material fulfillment.

Power is the first book to reveal how to contact, communicate, and work with the highest spiritual power and how to make that power available for the spiritual and material transformation of the individual and the world.

Twenty years of Eric Mitchell's spiritual quest have been synthesized into less than 200 pages, so that every student of spirituality and life can find here a treasure trove of wisdom and its practical use. These are directions to find your true home, the One Power. The great spiritual beings of the past changed our societies, but the transformation of human consciousness did not happen. This book presents a new approach to solving that problem.

0-87542-499-6, 192 pgs., mass market, illus.   **$3.95**

THE MAGICAL HOUSEHOLD
by Scott Cunningham and David Harrington
Whether your home is a small apartment or a palatial mansion, you want it to be something special. Now it can be with *The Magical Household*. Learn how to make your home more than just a place to live. Turn it into a place of security, life, fun and magic. Here you will not find the complex magic of the ceremonial magician. Rather, you will learn simple, quick and effective magical spells that use nothing more than common items in your house: furniture, windows, doors, carpet, pets, etc. You will learn to take advantage of the intrinsic power and energy that is already in your home, waiting to be tapped. You will learn to make magic a part of your life. The result is a home that is safeguarded from harm and a place which will bring you happiness, health and more.

0-87542-124-5, 208 pgs., 5-1/4 x 8, illus., softcover   **$8.95**

THE NEW MAGUS
by Donald Tyson
The New Magus is a practical framework on which a student can base his or her personal system of magic.

This book is filled with practical, usable magical techniques and rituals which anyone from any magical tradition can use. It includes instructions on how to design and perform rituals, create and use sigils, do invocations and evocations, do spiritual healings, learn rune magic, use godforms, create telesmatic images, discover your personal guardian, create and use magical tools and much more. You will learn how YOU can be a New Magus!

The New Age is based on ancient concepts that have been put into terms, or metaphors, that are appropriate to life in our world today. That makes *The New Magus* the book on magic for today.

If you have found that magic seems illogical, overcomplicated and not appropriate to your lifestyle, *The New Magus* is the book for you. It will change your ideas of magic forever!

0-87542-825-8, 368 pgs., 6 x 9, illus., softcover   **$12.95**

PRACTICAL SIGIL MAGIC
by Frater U∴D∴
This powerful magical system is right for anyone who has the desire to change his/her life! Frater U∴D∴ shows you how to create personal sigils (signs) using your unconscious. Artistic skill is not a necessity in drawing sigils, but honest, straightforward, precise intentions are, and this book gives samples of various sigils along with their purpose.

Based on Austin Osman Spare's theory of sigils and the Alphabet of Desire, *Practical Sigil Magic* explores the background of this magical practice as well as specific methods, such as the word method with its sentence of desire. The pictorial and mantrical spell methods are also explained with many illustrations. The last chapter is devoted solely to creating sigils from planetary cameas.

Once you've created your sigil, you'll learn how to internalize or activate it, finally banishing it from your consciousness as it works imperceptibly in the outer world. Let Frater U∴D∴, a leading magician of Germany, take you on this magical journey to the center of your dreams.

0-87542-774-X, 166 pgs. 5-1/4 x 8, illus., softcover   **$8.95**